**ESTEP & FITZGERALD
LITERARY PUBLISHING**

Confetti Covered Quicksand

BY
Amy Asbury

AUTHOR OF
THE SUNSET STRIP DIARIES

THIS IS THE STORY OF MY YOUNG ADULT YEARS
AS I REMEMBER THEM. ALL NAMES HAVE BEEN
CHANGED AND ARE COMPLETELY FICTIONAL.
SOME CHARACTERISTICS AND MINOR DETAILS
HAVE BEEN CHANGED.

Table of Contents

FOR KIM

One

WHEREFORE ART THOU,
O HAIR BANDS?

(Cue Radiohead's "Creep")

It was March of 1993. I was nineteen years old. I had spent the last three years in Hollywood, partying on the Sunset Strip with the hair bands. As most people who make a full time job of partying, I struggled with a difficult adolescence. My father was inappropriate toward me sexually and it was most likely due to the fact that he was a cocaine addict. My mother was depressed and wanted nothing to do with me. At about twelve, I started cutting myself with knives and pins. It went unnoticed.

At thirteen, I developed the old stand-by of girls who are trying to tell their parents they are in trouble, bulimia, but that shit didn't work. They didn't even notice sprayed barf on their toilets and my weight loss. At fourteen, I went to plan C: become the school 'bad girl.'

I wanted to look like Kelly Bundy; I thought she looked great. I wore tight clothes, high heels, lots of makeup and started flirting with boys. By the time I was fifteen, I was drinking bourbon to the point of passing out. I started hanging out with the older guys who cruised the high school looking for fresh meat. I found myself in far too many situations where I was waking up without my clothes on. One of those nights resulted in a humiliating videotape, which was used to blackmail me. As a consolation prize, I contracted a case of VD so painful that it brought me to the hospital.

My school finally called my mother and asked what in God's name was going on in my home. My mother had no choice but to get rid of my father. She divorced him and we moved into my Grandmother's house in Los Angeles's San Fernando Valley. That is when I decided I would rather be on the Sunset Strip in Hollywood, surrounded by other troubled people who wouldn't judge me. I just didn't know how I would get there.

I did my studies, which consisted of looking at hundreds of local magazines and listening to several hundred hours of music that sometimes sounded like dying cats. I learned what to wear, where to go, and who was in the "in" crowd. I went to get a tattoo (it sounded like a grand idea at sixteen) and after meeting the twenty-one-year-old tattoo artist, we started dating. He was friends with a lot of Hollywood people. I climbed on board through him, and then took it from there. After a year or two of playing my cards right and refusing to sleep with a few popular guys, I became the new "it" girl. I tried to hang on to it as long as I could, but then, just like all people who rise to the top, I began descending. And it wasn't just me, it was the scene in general. If you have watched VH1 any time in the last ten years, you will know that the sound of "Grunge" came into town in the early nineties and ended the hair band scene. It was quite a buzz kill.

Half of the people I normally partied with left Hollywood. They realized that their glam bands were being overlooked by the record companies and they returned to the states they came from with no record contract in hand. Others stayed in town and tried to adapt. They took off the tight pants, cut their hair a little and took off their makeup. It was weird to see the guys that had been in makeup and pink suddenly wearing lumberjack flannels and Doc Martens. There were a few guys that stuck to their guns and wouldn't change. With the exception of a few who made it in Japan, there was no place for them. They looked outdated and out of touch.

No matter what look they chose, the people who stayed seemed to be hitting the drugs. Many of them chose heroin. Some of the party crowd committed suicide. A few of the girls in our crowd started working for Hollywood madam Heidi Fleiss and others disappeared. There was a general scattering. I didn't know where that left me. That is the point where this story picks up.

So there I was, nineteen and washed out. I had just moved in with one of the girls that I was friends with in Hollywood, Missy. I was looking for a hostess job and headed into an Encino eatery called Pao Pao to grab an application. I took an escalator past potted palm fronds up onto a beautiful brick patio. Gorgeous people of both sexes were walking around with handled shopping bags. Everyone looked so...*manicured*. I saw Pao Pao first thing. It had huge glass doors. I walked inside and was immediately blinded by the sunlight pouring through the place. Half of the walls were glass, so they let in natural light. The other walls were mirrored. It was minimal and crisp looking with glass tabletops over white linen tablecloths. The servers were wearing burgundy colored aprons over white polo shirts with white pants. They all looked freshly showered and scrubbed. The place was the exact opposite of where I had spent the last three years of my life.

The next thing I knew, everything turned slow motion. This beautiful creature behind the counter looked up at me and we locked eyes. I saw thick dark eyebrows, smoldering honey colored eyes and short dark hair. He looked rather preppy, like a fraternity guy who played La Crosse or something. My life changed in that moment. Not that it changed me into a person who was suddenly doing charity work in St. John twin sets, but it changed me. I had been waiting for something to make me lose interest in the people I was keeping company with, but nothing was as interesting, so I kept going back. But now…now there was this new possibility…I actually found a normal looking guy attractive! I would simply start dating him, then-

tire screeching sound

It suddenly dawned on me. My shoulders dropped a little as I stood with the application in my hand and he went back to packing a 'to-go' order into paper bags. He wanted nothing to do with me. I looked at myself in the mirror next to us. My makeup suddenly appeared very heavy. My hair looked dull and brittle. I had gained weight from all of the late nights at Del Taco. I looked dirty and bloated. I did not know how to properly groom myself. I was no longer "fresh" or beautiful. I had become a sloppy drunk during my nights out with Missy. On any given night, I was slurring, foul-mouthed and ill-mannered with a complete lack of morality. I did whatever I wanted; indulged any behavior I felt like. I gave into any impulse I had.

There were times where that was awesome. If someone was an asshole, I said "you're an asshole" to their face, or slapped them. If someone did me wrong, I punched them in the nose. And hell, it was always great going to the store in my bright blue mud mask and pajamas. I didn't *care*. I did whatever I wanted, but I had no pride in myself. I was violent and abrasive, cursing and yelling at people, throwing food or bottles when I became angry. I fell over tables, out of car doors, danced on tables or bars and then came crashing down. I was an embarrassment. A total mess.

I left the restaurant in a slump and went home and watched *The Jenny Jones Show* and *Saved by the Bell* re-runs. A few days later, I got a call to come in for an interview. I drank some whiskey, which was perfectly acceptable in my head. How else would I be able to get through the interview? I drove my blue Honda Accord up to the beautiful, rounded little mall on Ventura Boulevard and pulled my car into the underground parking garage, where red-vested valets took my car and handed me a ticket. I went inside Pao Pao and met the manager who was to interview me. While he asked me questions, I couldn't help but stare at the clean-cut kids my age rushing around with trays of little dumplings and big round orbs of Chinese chicken salads. The manager asked me what my hobbies were and I started to squirm. Hobbies…*Well, I go*

*out with a bunch of guys wearing makeup and get so drunk
that I can't see straight. I also have a soft spot for drug
addicts and women in the sex industry...*

I ended up saying that I played tennis, which I had, in high
school. He nodded. I looked behind him. The restaurant
was so orderly and fresh and modern. One couldn't help
but feel in a good mood just being in a place like that. So
much sunshine and white everywhere. It was just what I
needed. No one was wearing black or smoking or being
violent. The clientele appeared upper class. I looked down
at what I was wearing. It was the only capable outfit I had:
a little short suit from Contempo Casuals. It had been my
sister's. It was a business-looking top connected with these
shorts that could pass for a skirt. It had sheer chiffon
sleeves and it was (whispers) *stapled together on one side.*
It was so hateful. The manager must have been partially
blind because he hired me as a hostess. I then had to wear
that outfit over and over until I could afford some new
clothes. The staples surely glistened in the bright sunlight
of that place.

I stood at my post at the hostess stand all day, opening
doors for businessmen and their lunching wives. I saw hair
that was highlighted; skin that was dewy and taken care of.
I saw tasteful manicures in hues of barely-there pink. I saw
soft leather handbags. I saw white teeth and delicate tank
watches. Men wore starched shirts and had shiny leather
shoes.

There were many TV stars coming in, mostly from the hit
show of the time, *Beverly Hills 90210*. Tori Spelling,
Tiffani-Amber Theissen and Kathleen Robertson
(remember Clare?) came in for Chinese chicken salads all

at different times. I would always try to eavesdrop on them while refilling their mango iced tea.

Baywatch was huge as well, and David Hasselhoff came in all the time with his little girls and beautiful green-eyed wife. He was always chatty with everyone and good natured. Lots of soap opera actors and actresses came in- I was always happy to see cast members of *Days of our Lives*. Random entertainment people like, say, Pat Sajak or the Wayans brothers came in. Joey Lawrence came in with his family quite a bit and even with his girlfriend of the time, Jennifer Love Hewitt. I remember one time they asked me about the gift-wrapped chicken on the menu. I was like, *Let's just say there is a **reason** that shit's gift-wrapped*...they thought it was funny. David Cassidy came in, as did some of the members of KISS and a couple of rappers. I saw lots of former child stars, newscasters and sitcom actors and actresses, all with their families. It was pretty cool.

When it got slow I would watch the waiters hustling around the floor in their crisp white uniforms. I fell into immediate lust with not one, not two, not three, but *four* of the waiters from Pao Pao. I had never seen such good-looking guys in the flesh. They were so different from the scrawny musicians with whom I had been keeping company. I was shocked at myself for finding these new guys attractive.

There was Shaun Peterson: huge and tan with dark blond hair past his ears and the lightest, pale blue eyes I ever saw. He had a big nose, but it suited him, and he was kind of a dick, but it was somehow hot. Shaun was an actor. He looked like he would play the bully, someone who picked

on the skinny lead character. It turned out that he played
exactly those parts. He had also posed nude for *Playgirl*. I
thought he was completely out of my league but loved
watching him and daydreaming. One day he told me I
looked like Jessica Rabbit and I nearly died. I went home
and danced around as if I was on hot sand with bare feet.

The second waiter was named David Duran. He was so
attractive I could hardly look at him. It was just *wrong*
how handsome this guy was. He had short dark hair and
dark eyes set into a chiseled face. He appeared to be a
deeply tanned white guy. He had a small part on *Days of
Our Lives*. I just remember he had huge biceps and was
tall. He had small features and a perfect smile. Kind of
looked like Josh Duhamel. He had a broken arm once and I
watched his muscles bulge as he balanced everything on
the other arm. He was the most obviously gorgeous out of
the four.

The third hot guy was named P.J. Clapp, also an actor. He
was from Tennessee and sometimes called himself Johnny
Knoxville at his tables. He did a little comedy routine by
putting on these Southern voices. Kids loved it. When he
sang happy birthday (as we all had to do for customer's
birthdays) he always did it in an Elvis voice. P.J. was tan
and tall with dark eyes; dark, ear-length hair that was
slicked back, and a perfect straight nose. He had movie
star good looks, but was not the typical actor. He was
definitely a weirdo. I felt the most comfortable around him
because he was laid back and funny- and he appreciated
my imitation of David Lee Roth jumping off a drum riser.
We was more my buddy after I got to know him better,
like a brother or something. P.J. subjected me to dozens of
stories about his weird skater and BMX type of friends and

I never really got what was so funny about half of the damn stories, but he was so cute, I laughed along with him. He did a reoccurring Mountain Dew commercial a few years later and then a show on MTV called *Jackass*, with his crazy friends. He became famous from his *Jackass* show and started doing real Hollywood movies, under the name Johnny Knoxville.

For some reason, the one I really fell for was the fourth guy: Jake Brenner. He was the kid who I saw the first day when getting the application; the one who I was sure had changed my life. Yes, he was stuck up, but I never saw a face like his. I was drawn to him. He was shorter than the other guys and was more my age. He wasn't an actor, he was just a rich kid. I never dated someone like that.

I became secretly obsessed with him. If I saw him flirt with girls, I felt nauseous. I had such a crush on this guy. One time the manager asked me to bring four drinks to one of Jake's tables. I had never balanced drinks on a tray before, so when I lifted up one glass of water to try to put it in front of a customer, the other three glasses came crashing down all over the table. He got to the table when I was trying to clean up the people. I could've died.

It was weird to lust after these guys and have them not be interested in me. I was so popular and pretty a few years prior that it was a shock to me that I ended up where I did.

Other things started to come to me as I spent my days around more "normal," if not well-bred people. I didn't know how to dress appropriately. I didn't know how to date or deal with the opposite sex in a natural way. I had no heroes, no influences, and no one to show me how to build character. I had no morals, no ethics, and no virtues. And as much as I wanted to blame it on the Hollywood crowd, none of it was the fault of anyone but me. It was all my own choices.

I felt self-conscious and stripped bare there in the daylight. Instead of trying to show off my Hollywood style, I wanted to hide it. I wasn't so sure that I was proud of it any more. I felt that maybe I was ready for something new, but I was too afraid to act on it. I didn't know how to *undo* everything I had done to myself. It would take a lot of willpower to change from my comfort zone.

Pao Pao hired a new waiter named Cameron. He was a little older than the rest of us and was very smart. He had been accepted into the film school at USC on scholarship. I was impressed. Cameron was brave. He was always laughing and very sarcastic. Shaun hated him and always tried to call him out for being gay, something Cameron never confirmed or denied- he simply didn't talk about it.

Shaun would come over with a red face and say, "So, are you going to go down to *Santa Monica Boulevard* tonight?" and Cameron would immediately push his buttons by bringing up his infamous *Playgirl* spread: "Did you think of that joke before or after you spread your butt cheeks in *Playgirl*?" (Shaun wouldn't talk about his *Playgirl* spread; he acted as if he were ashamed of it. We didn't know if he really was or pretending to be modest.) Shaun would then get mad and try to cut him down with another gay slur, but Cameron would only laugh and blow it off.

Cameron was quirky and not everyone took to him, like

when he would talk about his bowel movements, which grossed me out. "I just gave birth to three black babies!" he would say, thanking his prune juice. He rubbed a lot of people the wrong way, but I liked him.

I told Cameron about my former Hollywood nights, and how, on occasion, I still went and hung out at the clubs on The Strip. He was less than impressed. I thought for sure I could change his mind if I took him out with me one night; surely he would find it interesting or at least amusing.

I was wrong. He thought the people who were "left over" were hanging on to something that was dead. He thought I was partying too hard and too much. He thought I should stop going doing there; maybe try something a little less dangerous. I tried not to care, but he was the smartest person I knew, and he was in film school, something I wished I could be doing. I admired him. And I knew he was right.

I felt embarrassed. It made me uncomfortable. He was the only person who had ever said something like that to me. It kind of tugged at me. I knew there was no place left for me in Hollywood, but it was hard to let go of. There were people that transitioned out of that scene just fine; people that saw it as a fun party thing on the weekends. I was too manic to take it lightly like that; I was too entrenched. I always got too involved and ended up with no job, no place to live and bruises all over my body.

I knew I had to get a new crowd and a new hang out, stat. I grabbed the first thing in front of me: My co-workers. Just knowing that I could hang out with "normal" kids who had jobs and cars and who were my age was a relief to me. I always avoided it. I always thought they would be repelled by me; I wouldn't fit in; I wouldn't be able to relate to regular people and vice versa.

Being accepted by a nice group of kids made me feel good. Along with Missy, who I clung to desperately, they became my little family. While my young childhood was terrific, things crumbled in my teen years and by 1993, my original family unit was completely dissolved. My father was a full-time drug addict, my *sister* was a full-time drug addict, and my mother was in a blinding depression (she had said maybe four words to me in the previous four years.) They were people I once knew. I lost touch with all of my other relatives as well. I didn't even know them anymore. It was as if I had no background. I felt as if it were erased, like it never happened. I heard of other families saying that family was there for each other no matter what. That was not my experience.

What I learned from my family is that they would *not* always be there for me. It was every man out for himself. It was up to me to find a place to live if I had nowhere to go; to find food if I were hungry. I was truly on my own.

I had spent several years not thinking about my childhood, and it started to hit me around then just how much I missed it. I missed the time when my dad wasn't yet on drugs or being pervy; when my mother wasn't yet depressed. I wished things hadn't gone so wrong, that things could go back to the way they were when we were all okay, eating around our kitchen table and laughing. Thinking about it caused a pain so deep in my heart that it physically hurt me. I would take a bunch of pills and lay on the bathroom floor crying, just wanting to die. I couldn't believe how much I missed my old family, our old house, my old friends, and my old self. Hearing songs from that time stung. I wrote the following:

Journal Entry 9/12/1993

I have been going through some emotional shit. My mental health is not in good shape. I get sick to my stomach when I hear songs that remind me of the family I once had. I have been holding back tears at work when they play "Piano Man" by Billy Joel. It has been ten years. It is the ten year anniversary of the greatest time in my life. I haven't written about it, but I am completely and totally obsessed with it.

Last week I was screaming at the top of my lungs in my car, louder than I ever have, "I USED TO PLAY HANDBALL! I WAS IN THE FUCKING SCHOOL CHORUS!" It was so painful to remember who I used to be.

I don't know who I am any more. It hurts my heart so much to mourn my old self and my old family. I am completely separated from all of them. I just burst into tears again, over nothing. I am not doing so great with this misery hanging over me. I have never in my life felt so lost. Spending the past three years partying in Hollywood was pretty effective in helping me to forget about all of this stuff. I guess I am kind of faced with it all now.

When it got to be too much, I went and partied it up with the Pao Pao kids. We drank beer and smoked pot (which I had avoided until then) and listened to Rage Against the Machine, and Jane's Addiction's *Ritual de lo Habitual* album, which I was entirely sick of. If I heard the song "Stop!" one more time, I was going to stab myself in the eyeball. We were listening to all of the bands from that year's music festival, Lollapalooza. I had never partied with a crowd other than the one in Hollywood, so I kind of seemed like the crazy one of the group, just because of what I was used to.

The parties were sort of boring, but I didn't care: I was always hoping Jake Brenner would show up. One night he finally did, and we ended up making out in some bedroom. I was all thrilled for a day or two, until I got back to work and saw him and he completely ignored my ass. *Ouch.* I had not thought of what it would be like back at work! It was painful to be humiliated, but I sucked it up and tried not to think about it. I thought, *damn... 'normal' guys can be dicks too!*

Two

THE NANNY

I quickly moved up from hostess to working in the take out area, and then eventually to a waitress (cue *The Jeffersons* theme song). Jake Brenner finally left Pao Pao for college, and I went on with my life, which consisted of much drinking and tomfoolery. I had almost forgotten about him when he called me one day out of the blue and asked me if I would like to come spend the weekend at his parent's house in Santa Barbara the following week. I thought I would have a heart attack. I said yes.

The next day I panicked. Santa Barbara was like, two hours away. I didn't know how to get there. There was no internet back then (well, not in my world at least) and if you think I knew how to read a map, you are mistaken. If you were a girl driving by yourself in a car that would often break down and you had no bank account, no credit cards and no family to call (and there were no cell phones back then), it was scary to travel alone. But this was Jake Brenner! I had to go! There was no way I was going to say no.

Aside from the traveling alone portion of my worries, I became worried about the social aspect of the whole thing. How would I behave around his parents!? I was very uncomfortable around parents.

Part three of my worries was the fact that I was fat and faulty. I starved myself that next week and exercised every night by running up in the hills behind our duplex. Strangely, I actually looked slimmer after one week. I bought a little flannel top from Contempo (everything was flannel at the time, Grunge was in) that tied right under my boobs. I didn't think about how someone's parents would view that; I was still in that Hollywood mode of dressing to show off your body.

I pulled up to his parent's beautiful home on a Friday evening. I took a deep breath and knocked on the door. Jake answered, and immediately introduced me to his parents. I squinted my eyes as he kept reiterating that I was "really fun." His mother looked uncomfortable and his dad seemed more understanding. He was trying to show his parents that he wasn't serious about me, so they needn't worry. I was clearly not refined or poised. I was not girlfriend material. I had on too much makeup, wore inappropriate clothing and was basically a hot mess. I was not their kind and I knew it. I didn't know what to say to them. I hadn't been around parents for years, including my own. His mother looked terrified, but was polite. She showed me to the guest room, which was done in toile wallpaper and had frilly pillows on the bed.

We went out to some street fair that night, where the band X was playing. There was a mosh pit going on and I was sure to avoid it. We drank a ton of sangria, which made me have a huge headache the entire next day.

He wanted to go bike riding on the boardwalk at the beach that next morning and I panicked. I hadn't ridden a bike since my pink Huffy in sixth grade. Me on a *bike?* In the fresh *air?* Me, out in the *daytime,* period? I couldn't do it! But I couldn't let him know that. So, I wore my neon green stripper bikini top with shorts and rode on the crowded beach boardwalk with him. I crashed so many times! I literally crashed into people's *legs* as they were walking by! The bike was too high for me, so I couldn't maneuver it properly. I was wobbling around trying to stop the thing with my tippy-toes, while making sure my boobs didn't fly out of the bikini top, which they were known to do in those triangle tops. I remember thinking…*I can't believe I am here. Is this how normal kids live? This is madness!*

It was my very first time in a dating situation with a normal guy. A guy who had regular parents, a family home, and an education. I felt in over my head. It was so different from the Hollywood guys. You couldn't get much more opposite. My previous love interests had to wipe off their lipstick before making out with me or our lipstick would clash. They would do things like jump out of the car while it was driving, hang from second-story balconies, smash windows, and then shoot up some heroin after making out with another guy. We would wake up on the floor in a hallway of some building, in a heap. You think I am kidding- I am actually not. It was really like that. Dating protocol was something I was completely unaware of. I was a lot more comfortable in the chaotic situations, because that is how I was conditioned. That stuff I could handle. Bike rides and French toile wallpaper? Scared the shit out of me.

I realized on that trip that Jake was actually pretty insecure, and appeared to be worried about his weight and looks, not unlike a chick. I couldn't really fall for a guy who wasn't ballsy and confident. I was attracted to guys that didn't give a fuck- and he did. I was disappointed, but a bit relieved to be over my huge crush.

***

Journal Entry 10/10/1993

*I am depressed right now because I am at my mother's (she is not here) and the glorious pink bike I rode when I was ten is on its kickstand, right in front of my face! My sister and my mom (so sensitive, the two of them) tried selling my pride and joy for a measly ten dollars at a garage sale! There are so many things wrong with that sentence! And guess what? No one **bought** the thing! All the better, because now I can sit here and fucking stare at it and reminisce until I cry. Yes, this bike was one of the coolest things I ever owned. Ever. Now I wish it were gone so I wouldn't have to look at it and get upset.*

*My sister just got here. She says she is off drugs. Still, she is not like she used to be. She is very different. First of all, she **looks** like a completely different person. All that dark hair she had? Gone. She has this stringy, damaged, orange, non-color hair. The life has been sucked out of it. It looks terrible. She parts it down the middle and tucks the sides behind her ears. That is something people are doing this year, so I suppose she can get away with it. Anyway,*

*remember her potbelly and her dark skin? Forget it- she is
as thin and as white as a piece of chalk. I am not cutting
her down because I dislike her. She just really looks like
that. Very unhealthy. She actually looks better now than
she did! She isn't funny anymore, either. She used to be so
funny. The funniest person I ever met. To this day, when I
tell people stories of Becky, they laugh so hard that tears
come to their eyes.*

*She just graduated from high school, barely slipping by.
My mom didn't make much of a stink for her graduation at
all. As a matter of fact, during the ceremony she said she
was tired and wanted to go home and sleep! She didn't
hand Becky any flowers, take her to dinner, or even
pretend to be proud of her. She just looked depressed. She
got her a class ring some months before, so that is why she
didn't take her to dinner, I guess. She could have at least
given her some flowers for Pete's sake. But it's not like **I**
did anything either. Our childhood friend Karen was with
us and she actually went and stole some red carnations
from a table to give to Becky so she would at least have
something. Thank God for that. And of course, my dad
didn't even show up to see her, the bastard.*

I was still living with Missy, who was a cocktail waitress
at a strip bar at that time. Resentment started to build
between us around then. She was paying for most
everything: the food, the rent, the bills- I was chipping in
maybe $200 or $300 a month and then living off her and
letting her pay for everything else. I borrowed all of her
clothes and beauty products, used her phone, and ate her
food. I 'repaid' her by being the one with the car. I drove
her everywhere and often picked her up from work in
Hollywood and then drove us out to the clubs. Anyway,

we started to snap at each other when we were out drinking. She could have been resentful because she was always paying for everything, or it could have been a number of other things, who knows.

One night we had a drunken falling out, Hollywood style, which included the standard: full force kicking of my windshield and many flying f-bombs. It was a fight that we couldn't recover from. She either told me to get out of her house or I told her I was moving out- I can't remember. Then we told each other to fuck off.

I got all of my stuff into my car and drove to my mom's house. On the way there, I thought…shit…where am I going to live now? My mother was completely emotionally cut off from me. I knew if I asked her if I could stay, she would most likely say no. But I decided to ask her anyway. She had just had a hysterectomy and was laid up in bed. I proposed to her that I could pay some rent to her and also help her while she was bed-ridden.

She said absolutely not, it would be too much of a stress to have me there. I am sure it **would** have been stressful for her because yes, I was selfish and loud and a pain in the ass. But I truly had nowhere else to go. *Please. Please just let me stay here until I find something else, I will pay you; I will help you out.* She said no again. I stared at her. I wished all of the times she had hurt me in the past that I had just cried instead of becoming angry and full of rage, because then she could have seen how much she affected me. Instead, she only saw me behaving wildly irrational. This time was a little different. I didn't become violent, even though it felt like someone had poured hot lava through my veins. I was strangely in control. I told her I would be homeless; I had nowhere to sleep that very night. I was like, I am your daughter- your *daughter*- can I please sleep in your home until I find a place to fucking live?! *Please???* She looked up at me from her bed and told me to get some blankets and sleep in my car.

I took a deep breath.

"Sleep in my car, huh?"

I looked down at her in her bed and very calmly said,

"Can I ask you something? Who do you think is going to be taking care of you when you are old?"

I saw a splash of fear cross her face.

"What, do you think *Becky* is going to be able to take care of you? It's going to be *me*. So if I were you, I would be careful how you treat me."

Then I left. As pissed as I was, I didn't have time to sit there and cry about it; I had to find a place to live, and fast. I racked my brain.

Amelia. I will call Amelia.

Amelia Davenport was a friend of mine from high school. She was sort of frumpy and could be negative at times, but she was smart, witty, and a great confidante. I called her up and begged her to get an apartment with me. She said she would like to, but she needed a few months to save up. She still lived with her family, so she asked her mother if I could stay at their place. Her mother agreed. I was so glad somebody else's mother had pity on me!

Amelia's mother was a sturdy British woman who owned a clothing store. She paid all of the family bills. Her new husband, who looked sort of like Matt Dillon, was unemployed and living off her. I loved Matt Dillon, so I tried to distinguish any thoughts of viewing the stepdad as hot. I didn't want to cause any trouble.

I moved my duffel bag into their house, which was at the end of a cul de sac in Mission Hills, in the San Fernando Valley. They had a pool full of what looked like Koi fish, but Amelia said that they were just goldfish originally and they kept growing. It was rather disgusting.

I stayed at Amelia's for probably two or three weeks, driving myself to work in Encino while listening to my new Smashing Pumpkins tape over and over. Amelia's mother had some friends in from England who needed a nanny for their toddler, and she recommended me for the job. It sounded exciting, but I knew nothing about children. They didn't seem to mind. They said they would give me room and board as payment, and I could still keep my part time job at Pao Pao. The plan was for me to save all of my money for a month or so and then move out with Amelia at the beginning of the New Year.

I moved straight into the home of these total strangers named Charlotte and George. Charlotte was a character actress and could be considered homely. She was a tiny, dark-haired woman with a huge, gnarly, twisted nose; small lips and beady eyes. This sounds mean-spirited, but it was true: she played unattractive roles. Like, Tracy Ullman type of roles. She didn't mind being cast as an ugly person. You would think someone so gnarly looking would actually be really nice and surprise you, but not this person. She was quite negative and angry. She was always complaining about something.

Her husband George was short with a little weight on him. He had blue eyes, red hair and worked for a bank. Both of them spoke the Queen's English, these tidy British accents that I adored. They had one daughter named Elizabeth who was three years old. She was quite smart, but very bitter and unpleasant. She was incorrigible; just plain sour, with a little British accent and curly red hair. She also had a very pinched and unsightly look to her. She had so many toys and had everything she wanted, but she was awful. Now I realize that she was emulating her mother.

I didn't quite know what to do with Elizabeth. I played Peter Pan and 'don't touch the ground' with her; games I had played with my sister. It was kind of nice sometimes. One day I taught her the names of all of the gemstones and she picked them up right away. "Emerald! Sapphire! Ruby!" Her little dimpled hand pointed to each one in a catalog that came in the mail.

I initially liked the idea of Charlotte and George's. It was a real, live, warm home. They had unlimited food for me to eat, which was like heaven. I always chose the Cornflakes with icy cold milk and sugar sprinkled on top; it tasted like a true delicacy. Charlotte often made Shepherd's Pie, which was like a pie only it was made with meat, potatoes, peas, and then some mashed potatoes on top. I didn't much care for English cuisine, but I liked that it didn't include many vegetables. Charlotte tried to show me how to make tea one time and I couldn't get the hang of it. She said I was dreadful at it.

Most of the nights I lived there were spent in the guest bedroom, crying over my mother. I was so hurt by her that I couldn't get a hold of myself. Charlotte often barged in and asked me what in God's name was wrong and told me to pull myself together. I tried to explain the situation but only ended up crying more. She told me to forget about her and move forward. I nodded, wiping my snot.

The situation with Charlotte and George turned sour very quickly. I didn't know the standard rules of good behavior, so my manners were terrible and I offended them constantly. For one, I didn't know that most people come out and say goodnight before they go to bed. They were always offended that I just went to bed without the goodnights. They were also offended that I didn't come out and watch TV with them or chat with them. I didn't know what to say. I thought they would want me to give them their family time, but they wanted me to be more a part of the family. That was not something I was used to. I couldn't make myself open up to either of them, it was no wonder they didn't like me. It was all new to me and I was scared I would mess it up. I couldn't talk around them. I couldn't be warm. They didn't understand and grew to dislike me. Things started to become very strained, eventually blowing up.

I felt kind of trapped and felt like I had no privacy. The bursting through my bedroom door without knocking was wearing thin on me, and I was becoming irate that they didn't want me going out at night after my job. They wanted me to stay home and I wanted nothing more than to leave. I kept telling myself to hold out, only a few more months to go.

When I first arrived, the terms were that I would just take care of the child each day (I worked nights.) Then, slowly, they decided I should start housekeeping, which was probably because I wasn't pulling my weight in some way. Charlotte was speechless when she saw my cleaning jobs. She would say, "Who doesn't know how to *clean*? Don't you see that *dirt*?!" But I didn't. I was very messy. The next thing I knew, I was cleaning the place and taking care of Elizabeth with no breaks, non-stop. I was miserable.

I started sneaking out to a Beverly Hills nightclub called Bar One after they went to bed. This guy I met when I was much younger named Rich Ross had me on a guest list for the rest of my life. I was sort of a pimp though; I had to bring really pretty girls to the club, and in exchange, I would get free drinks and dinner and whatever I wanted. Rich would get pissed if I brought girls that were not up to his standards, as in not gorgeous and thin. And God forbid I put on weight myself. He would sit there with his Andy Gibb hair and running shorts (he always looked exactly the same) and eat his broiled lamb and say, "You know, sometimes people think they are fabulous... and they are not." Rich normally called me a bombshell, and told me I was "fan-tabulous," but when I started putting on weight, he would avoid me and throw attitude. He bought me many a dinner and drink at the Rainbow in my teenage years. Any time I walked through those doors, I could go sit at his table and order anything I wanted. I was usually starving, so this came in handy throughout my teen years. It was also coming in handy in my twenties.

Three

FEEL LIKE MEETING A PRINCE IN EUROPE ?

I had a good friend named Birdie Montgomery; I met her in Hollywood the previous year. She was three years younger than me, and really pretty. She was so pretty that it sucked, because I felt ugly next to her. She was always impeccably groomed with long, beautiful caramel hair in big loose curls; perfect makeup application and a cloud of Chanel perfume around her. She looked like a young Jessica Alba with huge boobs. She had sort of a snobby air about her and was quite prissy.

Birdie and I were partners in crime on the Sunset Strip during the hair band time period, and now we were both drifting off into a different territory: The L.A. club scene. It was chock full of celebrities, drugs, and general shadiness. It was really one of the worst places for a girl like Birdie to be. She was sixteen and bold; not afraid of anything, and very curious. I had slightly more sense than her, so I was often unable to relax when I was with her because I had to watch out for her. She was always getting into trouble, and not just typical teenage girl trouble.

A good example of this was one of the nights I snuck out of the house in order to go to Bar One with her. Heidi Fleiss, a former Hollywood madam, was in jail at the time but that didn't stop her boyfriend Ivan and some other junior apprentice from taking over her business right there at Bar One.

The junior apprentice was named Laurie. She had on light makeup, had shoulder length hair and was dressed very casually in an understated white t-shirt and jeans. I guess that was rule number one of the Madam Handbook: don't be too flashy. She did a good job of it; she was actually very forgettable, but incredibly confident. In hindsight, I think she was really just 'coke confident,' something I have seen all too much of in the years since then. It is when someone, after doing a few lines of cocaine, is a little too pleased with themself. They find themselves fascinating and they won't shut the fuck up because everything seems like such a *great* idea. One feels indestructible, like a super hero; everywhere they go is the place to be, everything they do is the thing to do. Yep, coke confident is what she was. She talked a little too much, bragged far more than was necessary, and generally had all of the other aforementioned traits. She seemed sort of juvenile- she was clearly new at what she was doing.

Anyway, I was too fat at the time, thank God, but Birdie was a perfect specimen of beauty and youth. They spotted her straight away and approached her for the hard sell. Their technique was based on the fairy tale dreams of most young girls: finding Prince Charming. They told her they had some prince lined up for her to meet and they wanted to send her to Switzerland (where he was staying) in order to meet him. They said she was his type; he would just *love* her, and who knows, she could end up marrying him. They said she didn't have to do anything she didn't want to do and it was all her call. At the very least she could enjoy Europe, see the sights and whatnot. I wouldn't have believed them from the jump because it sounded a little too good to be true, but the truth was that I recognized Ivan from the news; I knew he was an accomplice of Heidi's. They were open about it- I think I asked them, I can't remember, but they were open about taking over the business for the time being. Laurie said that she didn't see it as something bad. She considered herself in the matchmaking business; that she was just there to set up the right people and if love, marriage and the title of Crown Princess came later, then all the better.

Birdie sat there listening and looked at me, locking pupils with me. It was a look of hers that I knew too well. It meant: *I know this is going to get me into trouble somehow, but it sounds adventurous.* My look, one that I was having to bust out more often than I wanted to, said: *Oh no. No girl, no.* We went and huddled in a sidebar conference. She said she knew it sounded crazy, but wouldn't it be fun to go to Europe on their dime? And the prince, what if he really *did* like her? I forbade her to go. I said it was one thing to get into trouble here in town, but I wouldn't let her leave the country by herself; it was too dangerous. I couldn't watch over her. She would be alone. What if she ended up missing? Never seen again? I was sure I had heard a story or two about girls being sold into slavery or something equally awful. Lots of L.A. girls had gone over to the Sultan of Brunei, and the rumors were not pretty. I reminded Birdie that she still lived with her *parents*- what was she going to tell them? *Hey, I'm going to Switzerland, be back later?*

I saw the wheels turning in her head. She went back to Laurie and said she wanted to go, but on one condition: They had to let *me* come with her. They looked over at me (I was not only fat but I was wearing a fucking beret that night) and reluctantly agreed. I was like, wait- can we *discuss* this? I didn't have a good feeling about it, but thought that maybe with my street smarts we could somehow finagle out of any danger.

Ivan and Laurie were so smitten with Birdie that they wanted to wine and dine her (and her fat, beret-wearing friend as part of the deal.) They took us to some restaurant in Beverly Hills. As we were getting out of the car with them, a bunch of paparazzi started snapping pictures. Heidi Fleiss was a big news item at the time and so was anyone who was connected to her, apparently. I put my hand out to block the picture- I didn't want my face in the same frame as those two! Shit! I was pissed, but held my tongue. Once we got inside the restaurant and got settled, they continued their pitch on Birdie. They reiterated how glamorous it would be for her in Europe and how she could end up marrying royalty and spending the rest of her life in couture. She half listened to them, but seemed more interested in dipping her $20 fries into ketchup.

After the dinner, we piled into their silver Range Rover and Laurie put on the Nine Inch Nails song "Closer" (which I don't think was even released to the public yet) and sang along in a really intense and showy way. It was all very coke-ish, a word I had to invent just now to describe such antics.

They told us they were bringing us back to Heidi's place to party. *Heidi's place? Fuck!* I thought. Then I remembered she was in jail. Eh, I guess it wasn't a big deal just to go to her house if she wasn't even going to be there, right?

I was a bit drunk, as I always was, but I remember seeing a marble foyer and a marble bathroom with gold faucets, that I promptly used to pee in. When I was done with the bathroom, I joined them in a boardroom type of room, with a very long table surrounded by chairs. I wondered if they held meetings or something. It all looked so official. Ivan said he had to fax Heidi something and excused himself to the fax machine. She was allowed to use a *fax machine* in prison? Hmmpf. I looked at Laurie, her big mouth yapping away at Birdie, who looked bored. I wondered if Heidi purposely brought Laurie in to continue the business, or if she took over because there was an opening? At that moment, Birdie was done listening and was ready to start talking. I looked over with amusement to hear what would come out of her mouth.

"I am going to need a car. I can't even get anywhere, so this wouldn't work for me."

I straightened my posture and looked around. Where was she going with this?

Ivan didn't miss a beat. He said there was one downstairs that she could have. She asked if it was a stick, because she could only drive an automatic. He said it was indeed a stick, but, "if you can back it out of the driveway, it's yours."

We all got up and went to the driveway to see a beat up, brown Hyundai. I almost choked on my spit. What the fuck kind of car was *that*? What happened to their Range Rover? I expected there to be at least a BMW or at the *very* least a nice Toyota. But no: a dog shit brown Hyundai sat there, full of dust. Maybe it was the equivalent of wearing jeans and a t-shirt. Maybe it was to draw less attention? Or maybe it was the maid's or something? Before I could even figure that out, Birdie was in the driver's seat and Ivan and Laurie were standing by the car. She turned it on and tried working the clutch and the stick shift. The car jerked all over the place. I started to giggle. She kept trying to concentrate. Everyone was all serious. I put my hands over my mouth to stifle my laughter. The sight of her in that car was hilarious and then the fact that she couldn't even reverse the thing out of the driveway was even more awesome. Needless to say, she didn't get the car! And I eventually talked her out of going to Europe.

***

One night Charlotte received news of a death in the family, and it affected her terribly; she was screaming and crying. I stayed in my room; I didn't know the proper thing to do. I didn't want to do or say the wrong thing. I decided that I should leave and let her be alone with her friends and family that were coming over. I figured that the last thing she needed was *me* there, someone who annoyed her so much. But it turned out, staying in your room and saying nothing at all is rude and so is trying to leave. She was offended that I was leaving and started screaming at me. She screamed that I couldn't go anywhere until I cleaned the den. I knew she was going through a rough time so I didn't engage in her an argument, I just said "later" and burst out the front door.

I am sure I wasn't cutting it and did a terrible job and was rude myself. I had no manners to speak of and was surely offensive to the family. I probably had no idea how lazy I was being and how little housework I was actually doing. I was getting free room and board- I really had some nerve coming home at all hours in the morning, hung over, to take care of a child the next day.

I should've been more grateful and worked a lot harder, but I was too young and foolish to understand. I didn't know the correct behavior during her time of grievance. I didn't know to say "I am so sorry" or "Is there anything I can do?" or just help out and take Elizabeth aside so she could mourn. I wish I had handled that differently. I never touched anyone, hugged anyone, offered sympathy, or had any empathy. I was a very cold person and had been for some time. I just didn't know how to be warm with people.

It was about mid-December in 1993. I was working with hot Shaun Peterson a lot and he was playing the role of big brother, listening to my problems regarding my living situation. He was renting a huge house off of Topanga Canyon (over the hill from Malibu) with some of the other guys from work. I had partied there several times and knew the guys who lived there pretty well. Shaun said that I could stay with them if need be; the door was always open and to just come on over if I needed to. The night I left my job as a Nanny, I drove straight to his house.

I felt great relief being out of Charlotte and George's

house. Then it hit me- I was going to be living with four guys. At first, I was worried about looking pretty. I thought, *I can't let these guys see me without my makeup!* But I knew it would be a very small price to pay to have a roof over my head.

My new neighborhood was a sleepy area filled with dripping trees and hidden homes. It was sprinkled with miniature restaurants, tiny boutique shops and a little general store.

Shaun's place was set very far back from the street at the end of a long driveway. You couldn't even see the house from the street; it was hidden by trees. The place had hardwood floors and barely any furniture, so it echoed. It had a step-down dining room and a large tile kitchen with a balcony that jetted out over rooftops and trees below. The backyard was on a hillside. There was a pool and lots of white Greek statues and pillars, a thatched-roof tiki bar with sinks, and a bench in the very back underneath a huge, shaggy pepper tree, where people sat and smoked pot. The yard was gaudy and fabulous, downright perfect for a bunch of twenty-somethings. Everyone liked to stand on the patio at night and drink beers while looking out over the twinkling lights of the San Fernando Valley.

I slept on the scratchy living room couch with some blankets. I remember always being cold and hoping I didn't get scabies, which is always the worry of someone sleeping on a party couch. I had a cheap drug store alarm clock to wake me up for my shifts at Pao Pao. One of the girls at work who I normally hated, Courtney Salzberg, brought me a beautiful and plush goose down comforter to use. I was very grateful and never forgot it, even though she and I fought later on down the line. I could never really hate her because she was kind enough to let me have that luxury from her home.

As for the four guys I was to live with, there was Shaun; he was still an aspiring actor and still had huge light blue eyes, tan skin, longish dark blond hair, and a hot face. I shook my head like there were marbles in it to stop myself from thinking about him posing nude in Playgirl. Luckily, he took on a paternal role. He announced to the others that I would be staying with them as long as I needed to.

Then there was a guy named Anthony Rivera, who was an employee at another Pao Pao location, but partied with everyone at the Encino location. He was a short, funny, gay Latin guy who had slicked back hair. He was really crazy so I hung out with him a lot. He was a good five or six years older than the rest of us and sold cocaine out of the other location's take out area. The code word was something like "I'll have a diet soda" and he would sell you a bindle. He got so into it, that one time someone really *did* want a diet soda and they got some cocaine instead. But back to the story…

My third new roommate was tall, German Tim Schmidt. He was outgoing and smart with big soft blond curls in his hair, blue eyes and wire rimmed glasses. He wasn't my type, but he got chicks. We partied together a lot. He dressed like sort of a hippie, wore Patchouli, and smoked pot. He was really into music, mainly anything that was played at Lollapalooza. He had lots of paisley and Indian print stuff in his room.

Lucas Hoffman was the fourth guy who lived there. He

had long, straight blond hair and sort of a pug nose. Chicks dug him because he looked like a rocker, but I had had enough of that look. Lucas rarely spoke. I swear he may have said ten words the whole time I knew him. Anthony always made jokes about how hot Lucas was, so Lucas tried to get him to clean his room and shit. Anthony would say, "This Mexican does not run after you, *white boy.*"

Shaun, Tim, Lucas and I lived in the main house and Anthony lived in a little guest house off the garage, and that was good, because he would blast Wham so loud that the neighbors would call the cops. He was reading a lot of Anne Rice at the time, so he named his new kitten Lestat. Lestat was a little black fluffball who Anthony insisted was gay. He would say, "Move your tail to the left if you are straight and to the right if you are gay, Lestat," and the little pile of puff would move his tail to the right.

One day I was taking out the trash and I lifted up the trash can lid. Something was rustling deep inside the can. I dug underneath some trash and found a Kentucky Fried Chicken box that was completely closed, yet moving around. I was like, *Lestat? Is that you?* I opened the box and there was Lestat, all full of grease and licking his chops. He was so gross from the trash can that I had to carry him by the scruff of the neck. Then he farted. I shut my eyes and shook my head, and brought him to Anthony. He took him and dunked him in the pool and scrubbed him.

One day Shaun decided that I should have an actual room instead of sleeping on the couch. The guys all helped to build a wall across the wide dining room, complete with door. I was impressed that they even knew how to do it.

After a month or so, another of our co-workers moved into the house to cut our rent down. His name was Blake Martin and he was maybe a year younger than me. He was tall and handsome from certain angles; he looked a little bit like a young Tim Robbins. He was always doing unfunny *Jerky Boys* and *Beavis and Butthead* imitations and he usually annoyed the shit out of me because he acted pretentious- he was always bragging about things and acting cocky. I had to be nice to him though, because he was the only one with a TV in the damn house and he kept it locked in his room. That was the type of guy he was.

Blake had this little girlfriend named Ursula, who looked no older than ten. I relentlessly made fun of him for dating her. He said he was with her because her family had money, and then proceeded to put *me* down for not having any. He said he could never date me because I was too 'blue collar' and I had split ends and my nails weren't in good shape.

No one had said that to me before. That must have been why I hadn't attracted the hot waiters at Pao Pao. I looked... *blue collar*? What did that mean, exactly?

Blake was a source of hurt and also someone I wanted to conquer. As the months went on, I started falling for him. I was so mad at myself. We had a full-blown affair and I told no one. I couldn't let Anthony find out because he thought Blake was such a tool and thought I agreed. The problem was that I DID think he was a tool. A hot tool. Maybe one of those hot welding irons or something. Regardless of my bad judgment, his comments affected me.

A pretty girl named Molly was hired at Pao Pao around that time. She was a beautiful sorority girl, who was also very kind. I didn't know if she came from a well off family; her manners led me to believe she did, even if her car was a total clunker. She was tall and thin with the face of an angel: a pretty upturned nose, pouty lips, huge child-like eyes and long, shiny golden hair. She didn't need a drop of makeup. She never looked down on me and was friendly to all of the guys in the house, who were falling all over themselves when she came over to hang out with me. She was so gorgeous, that even Lestat had a crush on her. He lay on his back and looked up at her. She put her face down toward him to coo at him and he looked into her eyes and put his paw on her cheek and stared at her. It was the weirdest thing. And even stranger than that, when she tried to go home he jumped onto her windshield. He wouldn't get off her car. He didn't want her to leave! She kept laughing and saying, "Lestat! I have to go! I will come back and see you, okay?" He was in love. It was no shock that she put him under a spell. I pictured her with cartoon birds fluttering around her and a deer at her feet as she sang in the forest and shit.

Molly was so sweet, that it was a huge shock to all of us when all she wanted to do was smoke everyone's weed. One day Tim wasn't home and she suggested we go through his things to find his stash. I shrugged and said, *sure, why not?* We looked through all of his hippie stuff and sure enough, she found a baggy inside some Indian box. We sat right there in his Patchouli scented room and smoked all of his shit. She told me about dating a famous musician when she was thirteen years old, along with a lot of other interesting stuff. I found her fascinating.

After we got stoned, we went into my room. I had magazine covers taped to the wall. She very nicely and gently made a suggestion to me: *Why don't you frame those? Find some really cute frames and paint them white?* She said they would look a lot better that way. I confided in her about my lack of knowledge in the area of decorating and good taste in general. Being stoned, I added in that I was embarrassed that I didn't have any clothes of good quality. She went to my closet and looked at the four or five poorly made outfits I owned. She looked at the labels, which were very inexpensive brands and suggested I cut the tags off.

After she left, I fell onto my bed and put my feet on the wall. I felt a little saddened. I suddenly understood what Blake was saying. I was trashy. I didn't know how to decorate. I didn't own nice clothing. My heart sank. It was if I had been walking around in public with toilet paper on my foot. I had never entertained the thought that I was seen as someone from a lower social class than others. I didn't ever consider that one's belongings or one's grooming showed such things. It was another part of life that hurt me, but I knew it was something I couldn't stop. The judgment of others would always be there. I had been riding on my looks through my teenage years- social class was completely null and void. Just the idea of the words 'white trash' and 'blue collar'- I didn't know how to get my head around it. I knew something had to be done about it, I just didn't know what.

***

For the most part, we all got along pretty well in the house, but there was a little bit of tension between the responsible (Shaun) and the irresponsible (Anthony). Anthony felt that Shaun was looking down on him for drinking and partying so much. He was right. Shaun *was* disgusted by Anthony's drug and alcohol abuse, but let him move in because he needed another person to cover the rent on that huge house. I understood how Anthony felt because Shaun could stare at you and make you feel like shit.

Shaun pulled me aside one day at work. He asked me how much I made a year, and I told him it was about $6000. He told me that was below the poverty line. He asked me what I wanted to do with my life and I didn't have an answer. I told him I used to be ambitious as a kid, but at that point in my life, I was just trying to survive. He grilled me a little bit. He said I needed a dream, something to shoot for. I told him that my family was all jacked up and I had no support and there was no way I could amount to something. Shaun told me something that I never forgot. He told me a story about identical twins that grew up in really poor, shitty, abusive circumstances. One grew up a bum who was addicted to drugs and the other grew up to be a very successful millionaire. They were both asked why they had turned out the way they did. Shaun looked at me with a serious look on his face and said, "They both gave the same answer. *It is because of the way I was raised.*"

His concern made me uncomfortable- I didn't want to deal with bettering myself. I ignored his advice and sided with Anthony, who talked behind Shaun's back and made fun of him. I had no loyalty. It was as if he had never helped me; never taken me in when I was in need. He eventually moved out to get away from us losers. He told me I could take his old room- the master bedroom. It was the coolest room because it had its own bathroom and sliding glass door to the pool. The other three guys had to share a bathroom (Anthony had his own in the guesthouse.)

Anthony started working for a movie production company around then, as an assistant director. There was a lot of down time between projects, so he was often laying around the house drinking beers. He often told me hilarious stories about his dates, or , er, *tricks*. One time he went home with some "Old Bones" to try and make some rent money, but all the guy did was buy him some Kentucky Fried Chicken (which he apparently still liked to eat) and dump him back off on the street. Anthony looked at me with his eyebrows up and a Coors Light in his hand and said: "It was extra crispy girl. *Extra. Crispy.*" He talked about going home with guys after the clubs. He would often steal their cologne bottles, hats and other trinkets when they went to take a shower after hooking up with him. He had a huge cologne collection and needless to say, the fucker always smelled good.

If Anthony saw a hot waiter when we were out to eat, he always took his napkin, tucked it in his shirt, grabbed his knife and fork and said, "LUNCH." Or if there were young, hot high school guys, he said, "School is OUT." I was very amused by him and found myself laughing more than usual. Sometimes he went in the bathroom and ratted his slicked back hair out into a huge afro, standing a foot off his head in all directions. He would come into a room where I was reading or something and he would put his hand on his chest and say, "Girl, I got shocked real good," and pretend he had just been electrocuted, out of breath and thankful to be alive. I always got a kick out of that shit.

Random people and animals were always walking through

the front door of the Topanga house, which was never locked. When a pizza delivery boy came to the door, Anthony always dragged him inside and gave him beers. One day I was sitting there reading and two dogs ran right past me in the living room and out to the backyard. I went back to reading my book. Another time Anthony was lying by the pool and he felt someone staring at him. He put down his *Interview* magazine and saw that a drooling black Rottweiler was sitting there staring at him. There was always something crazy happening at that house.

Four

EARTHQUAKES AND RAGERS

It turned 1994. The movie *Reality Bites* came out and that Lisa Loeb song "Stay" was big. The Cranberries, the Gin Blossoms, and Beck were popular. Anthony loved that "Mmmm mmmm mmmm" song by the Crash Test Dummies. There was some new R & B stuff out, like Da Brat's "Funkdafied," Coolio's "Fantastic Voyage," and Aaliyah's "Back and Forth." Ice Cube put out "Bop Gun" and Queen Latifah came out with a song called "U.N.I.T. Y" which I loved because she yelled *'Who you callin' a bitch?'* in the background. The popular TV shows of the time were *Murphy Brown, Home Improvement, The Nanny, Mad About You, Seinfeld* and *Frasier*, none of which I watched.

I missed Missy; my life was so boring and lifeless without her. I called her and we made up. I figured that things would be better between us when we didn't live together (read: when I wasn't mooching off her.) I felt lost without her. She was so warm and comforting, smelling like vanilla, with this beautiful smile that just lit up my heart. I wanted to shrink her and make her into a doll that I could cuddle with at night. I know, I was crazy. (laughs). Our friendship survived the fight and we picked back up where we left off. We started going out on the weekends again and I often invited her over to party with the guys at the house. We had lots of laughs with Anthony and the others, who found her a lot of fun.

When I was through laughing and went into my room at night to go to sleep, I had my worries. I knew I drank too much. One night I drank so much that I threw up blood. Another night I woke up to find that I had pissed in my bed. I did everything to excess and did not take care of myself and that is because I hated myself inside. I also looked like shit: my hair was damaged because I couldn't afford good products, my skin was broken out because I couldn't buy good makeup and I had weight on me because I ate for comfort. Nothing felt better than eating a Tombstone pizza and drinking some fruit punch Gatorade. I knew my looks were no longer carrying me and I was newly aware that I came off as poor white trash. But there was one thing that bothered me more than any of that. *I didn't know what I was going to do with my life.* I was scared. How would I ever support myself? I didn't have enough money saved to get me through one *week*, let alone a year. I didn't know what to do about my future. I couldn't imagine *having* a future. I wasn't sure I would be alive. I wished I knew some adults- someone who could tell me how to do things. I was flying by the seat of my pants and I didn't know how long it would last.

That January, Anthony, Missy and I were out at a disco club in Hollywood called Club Seventies (it was held in the building that formerly hosted Riki Rachtman's club, the Cathouse). We got back home at around 3 a.m. I tumbled into the bed with Missy and Anthony took the couch. About an hour later, I awoke to the loudest rumbling sound I had ever heard. I am talking a sound that is not normal; a sound you've never heard before. My first thought was that it was an attack from another country- that we were being bombed. Before I could even form another thought, Missy jumped on top of me and shielded me while the TV came flying at us. She started screaming. It was an earthquake. A BIG earthquake. It was really dark and loud and the floor was violently shaking. Things were flying off the walls and we heard crashes coming from the surrounding duplexes. The wall fell off Missy's bathroom and her bathtub was exposed to the world. The collection of empty Jim Beam bottles on top of her fridge was shattering everywhere and so did the aquarium in the living room.

As the shaking started to calm down I put my contact lenses on in the dark. I immediately grabbed tennis shoes and sweatshirts and filled a duffel bag. I wanted to be prepared if we were going to be stuck outside. We wondered if Anthony was okay in the living room- we didn't hear any noise from him. *ANTHONY!* We screamed. No answer. *ANTHONY!* No answer. We looked at each other. Shit. Was he smashed to death? We crept out into the living room and saw his bloated body on the couch. His eyes were closed and his mouth was open. I covered my mouth and she continued to call his name. We were prepared to burst into tears when he started snoring like a pig. Could he have possibly slept through an earthquake that big? No fuckin way...

Yes fuckin way. Anthony was so drunk off Coors Light that the bitch slept through the big one. Glass shattering around him, broken trees, and collapsed buildings. None of it woke him up.

We all went out into the courtyard with the other neighbors who were all in pajamas and nightgowns and in different states of shock. One man was bleeding very badly and a little boy had crapped his pants. Anthony was still so drunk that he said, "It smells like SHIT around here," and proceeded to sniff big whiffs in an exaggerated manner. I elbowed him as the boy's mother took her son under her arm. Anthony suggested to the small crowd that we should loot. "I'm Mexican- you all better watch your hubcaps," he said, cackling. No one thought it was funny. He looked at me, shivering and looking down at the ground. "Are your lashes still on, girl? Where is your lip gloss? This calls for lip gloss! Earth tones girl, *earth tones*!... I need a motherfuckin beer." We ignored him. He got up and went in the house and dug through debris to find a beer and came back drinking one.

I was so scared. I was afraid to drive back to the Topanga house. When I finally decided it was safe to do so, I took Ventura Boulevard the whole way instead of getting on the 101 Freeway. I didn't want to be on some suspended bridge and have the whole thing come crashing down. Ventura looked terrible. All of the glass was shattered out of the windows of the stores; cars were smashed by trees.

When I got back to our house, Blake had a bunch of candles lit. I told him, *hey idiot, you aren't supposed to light matches during disasters because there could be a gas leak.* I wondered to myself if he had gotten the news that you shouldn't stick metal objects into light sockets. Our water and power was out for several days. After a week passed, I wondered if my mother and sister were okay. I hadn't heard anything. I couldn't get a hold of them. I finally got a hold of my grandmother who told me they were okay. I told her to tell them I was alive, if they asked.

Journal Entry 1/27/1994

My main fears right now are earthquakes, the rapture, death, hell, AIDS, not having a place to live in the future, scabies and chlamydia. I have a sinus infection. I need my teeth bleached, liposuction, and a nose job. I can't even think of anything that I like, except for the movie Peter Pan. *It comforts me more than anything else can right now. The songs, and the rooftops and chimneys against the dark sky; the warm nursery where the children are safe and tucked in their beds, sleeping in their pastel nightclothes with a big dog to protect them while their parents kiss them goodnight. I know it sounds crazy but I wish I could have all that more than anything else in the entire world.*

I hate that my family won't have me. I hate that I don't have any one true confidante. I hate that I gossip so much. I am still scared to grow up and become an adult. I wish I could be little again. I was so creative. When you are twenty years old, you can't exactly go climb on the woodpile or go out to play on the grass. I am in a crusty green robe, staring at a crummy glass of blush that will only give me a headache, should I decided to drink it. I feel like I am going to punch someone in the eye. I want to knock someone's block off or maybe just kick the wall 300 times so my foot will break. If I have to knock Shaun's cat off me one more time, I am going to go crazy. If I could break a plate over someone's head or something, I would feel relief. I just heard a real classy burp from that chump, Lucas. I hear Anthony doing one of the most irritating things he does besides snoring: whispering words out loud when he is reading.

*I just smacked a roley poley bug with my pen and it curled into a ball. I am looking at our end table. It has five different candles on it. A few are lit. There are two beer bottles of Bud Dry (1/2 full) and one can of Anthony's favorite, Coors Light (empty). There is a big seashell being used as an ashtray (full), a pack of Zig-Zag rolling papers, a book of matches from Jerry's Famous Deli, a big coffee table book on Rio and two different magazines with Playmate of the Year Anna Nicole Smith on the cover (*Playboy *and* Los Angeles.*) There is an empty carton of Ben and Jerry's frozen yogurt, complete with spoon; a bag of half-eaten pork rinds, a leather organizer, and a paperback book (mine) called* Even Cowgirls Get the Blues. *Cheap Trick is playing on the CD player and a few lights are on. The fucked up, brown, seventies furniture looks outdated. It is as cold as ever and all the guys are sitting around in shorts, reading books and magazines, scratching themselves in various places. Itch...scratch... itch...scratch...turn the page. Anthony just said: "Do you want some speed? Something to help you clean the house? If you did a couple of lines of coke you would be writing in hieroglyphics."*

Journal Entry 3/17/1994

I keep waking up in the middle of the night, thinking about how I will have nowhere to go in six months, when this lease is up. What if I don't even have a job? I keep thinking, wow, I am twenty years old and I have got to start doing all this stuff myself. There is no dancer to pay my way, no parent to protect me. It's just me and it is scary. I just looked down at my crotch and realized I have a huge rip in my pants.

The styles are considerably different now. No more scrunchies and big hair and loud colors. I think the biggest thing that has changed for women is the shape of the eyebrows- from unkept and thick to thin and arched. The color scheme is a big change as well: The girls all wear earth tones like beige, cream, and brown. Flannel shirts are still in style and those beige Timberland hiking boots with white socks and cut off denim shorts or skirts. The makeup is in neutrals: brown lip liner or lipstick, brown blush, straight hair parted down the middle and those damn tight dresses in small earth tone stripes that go down to the ankle. Courtney Salzberg wears those with little platform Converse and no socks, and manages to look cool. Girls are wearing "body suits" that snap in the crotch, with light denim jeans and chokers around the neck. Some girls are piercing their belly buttons and others are piercing their noses or tongues.

Guys are growing their hair out into bobs, kind of long on top and slicked back or hanging down around the ears. Some have hair to their shoulders and everyone is growing goatees. They have little hoop earrings or black string necklaces. Tattoos are more popular amongst mainstream guys- it's not just musicians any more. Everyone seems to be marking their bodies somehow or poking holes in themselves.

Jane's Addiction and Pearl Jam seem to be the thing these guys at work are into. Especially Tim, who reminds me of my father when he would get into his music. They go into a trance and ignore you. You ask them a question and they are waiting for a special part in the song where they can play the air drums, which they do right over your question. They maintain eye contact with you while singing or playing air instruments, but completely ignore the fact that you are trying to communicate. That is how most musicians are as well, which is maybe the reason I always tried to conquer them. Maybe they reminded me of my dad, ignoring me for music.

I am sitting in a community college class, trying to get my life together. There is a totally spun girl sitting next to me with red hair, blue eyes, bad skin, and a very thin frame. She is so clearly tweaking on something. She keeps telling me she wants to go out. At first I felt like inviting her out but then I realized she really has something to prove. She is always telling me really shocking stuff (which, of course, I have either heard of already or have done myself) to try and make me flinch. Maybe that is how I used to sound to other people. I remember feeling desperate to tell someone what was going on in my life, just because it seemed unbelievable sometimes. But I also got some sort of pleasure out of shocking people. I think that is where this girl is at.

When I went to this college a few years back, this weird, quiet girl and her mother were taking the aerobics class I was in for P.E. I noticed that the girl, rather average in looks and body-type, seemed to think she was the shit and

*couldn't be bothered with the mere laypeople around her.
Her mother was always whispering to her and they seemed
like they were hatching a plan to blow up the earth or
something. I glanced over at them from time to time while
grape-vining in my Reeboks, but other than that, I stayed
away from their sneaky secretiveness. When the semester
ended, they approached me outside the gym. The daughter,
who was my age, came to me and said she had a
proposition. Her mother, kind of shabby and frizzy-haired,
stood behind her prized offspring.*

*"I am looking for very rich, successful men," said the girl
very seriously, as if it she were the first person to come up
with such a plan, "and I need someone to accompany me
to exclusive events, restaurants and night clubs. My
mother and I think you would be perfect for the job. Now
remember, we are looking for the richest, most exclusive-"
I stopped listening and my eyes glossed over. I thought,
'bitch, this is the oldest, most played out idea in this town.
Did you just fall off the turnip truck?' I tried not to laugh
at her, because she was so serious. I told her that I grew
up in Los Angeles and all of that stuff was not my cup of
tea. I told her if she wanted to go to some cool events or
clubs, I would get her on a guest list through Rich Ross or
something, and then wished her the best of luck.*

*Speaking of Rich Ross, I haven't been accepting any
invitations from his secretary or press girl, or whomever it
is that calls me, so he has been calling me in person rather
than having her do it. He is pressuring me to go out with
him again. I don't want him to see I have put on weight.
His invitations to clubs and events will cease. His company
is throwing some Save the Surf benefit on Melrose next
week. I need to get it together so I can show up to these*

things and feel like I have some sort of a life.

Apparently, my idea of having a life was becoming something I hadn't tried yet: a fag hag. If you are gay, please don't be offended at my use of the word "fag"- I say it with love, ya big ol' queen. And while there may be no more use for the word 'fag' in today's society, there is still a need for hags. Who else will you drag around with you when your guy friends are out trolling for men and won't hang with your sorry ass? Us hags, that's who.

Okay, so, Anthony started taking Missy and me to the West Hollywood gay bars with him. We were on the lookout for new, fun things to do and were thrilled to go to these crazy clubs with names like "The Manhole" and my favorite, "Does your Momma Know?" We also frequented the usuals, Mickey's and Rage. I faintly remember standing at the bar at Mickey's and every time the bartender put down a drink for the waitress to deliver, I took it and dumped it into my own drink really quick. They caught on and threw me out of there so fast that I caught air.

It was kind of a relief to go to the gay bars. The guys weren't into us, so we could just laugh and dance. We would get really tanked and then go out to eat afterwards (Anthony always paid for all of my drinks and food.) We even came along with him to the Gay Pride parade. You would think a huge gathering of shirtless gay men would be like heaven to any gay man, but was actually a source of much hurt for the guys who were not totally chiseled and buff. Gay men in L.A. are, well, perfect. There is a lot of competition, because all of the hot gays from the other states come here- and it was no different in 1994. Anthony was short and not in shape, so he was upset that he couldn't snag a hot guy. They were all going for the *other* hot guys.

Many people wrongly think that all gay men are automatically attracted to all other gay men- that isn't true. They have types. There are white guys that only like Latinos. There are Latinos that only like black guys. And it isn't just race- there are guys that only go out with young guys, guys that only go out with tall guys; it's the same shit as women, really. They don't want fat asses, they don't want old asses (unless they are into daddies), and they don't want hairy asses (unless they are into bears.) There is surely some name for guys who like fat guys, but I don't know what it is and I am not about to Google it and get a bunch of gay porn viruses on my computer.

Back to the story. A co-worker of mine named Theodore started joining us in our clubbing. He was very obviously gay, but was afraid to come out of the closet. There is nothing more frustrating, let me tell you. We could see that this person's life would be so much better if he would just be himself, but he was terrified that he would be rejected by everyone in his life if he were to admit his lifestyle choice. And it just simply wasn't so! After what seemed like light-years, he finally sat us down and said he had something to tell us. He was practically shaking. He told us he was gay and then sat there sweating and shifting in his seat, looking like he was going to pass out. We said something like *Oh, is that right? Wow. What a shock.* I yawned and was like, *Are we done here?* and Anthony looked at his watch and said he was missing happy hour. Theodore looked back and forth at us and was confused. "Whawt? You guys saspected I was gaaay?" And mind you, this guy was doing kick ball changes and jazz hands while mouthing all the words to "Mr. Vain" in an exaggerated fashion. We said, "You? *Nawwww!*" I was thinking *girl please.*

After that, Anthony and Theodore were always on the prowl for fresh meat. Sometimes they would get on each other's nerves and get into a fight, which always entertained me. One night Anthony pulled down a huge palm branch that was hanging from a palm tree. Theodore was yelling at him and was moving his head side to side and putting his finger out and wagging it, totally doing that "Oh no you di-ent" move. Anthony started trying to beat him with the palm branch and Theodore was trying to push him. They were staggering all over the place in the dark and throwing random pieces of vegetation at each other. I was like "Ladies?! Can we wrap this up?!"

It was Theodore's birthday a few months later and Missy and I decided we would surprise him. We went and got a big box from behind an appliance store that had once held a washing machine. We brought it home and wrapped it in paper. Then we got in bikinis, made some "Happy Birthday" sashes, went to the liquor store, and bought a brand new bottle of bourbon to surprise him. We parked around the corner from his house, and untied the box from the roof. We were trying to figure out how we would get into it. We decided we would have to put the box over our heads and pop through the top of it once we got to his door. We had to let our feet stick out the bottom so we could walk up to his house. It was still light out and cars were passing by, honking. We got nervous. "Maybe we should just have a little sip of this," I suggested. The next thing we knew, we drank half of the bottle and were giggling and slurring. We tried walking with the box over our heads but we kept falling over and bumping into things because we couldn't see.

Theodore still lived with his father, mind you, but he was one of those "cool" dads. We somehow got up the steps to the door, rang the bell, and then crouched in the box. We heard the door open but we couldn't hear who opened it. Missy whispered, "Let's just jump out and say surprise now." We tried to jump, but the force of both of us just knocked the damn box forward into the house. We slammed onto the hard wood floor with the half-empty bottle of booze. When we looked up, we saw two grandparents and several older aunts and uncles. Theodore was behind everyone, looking at us with a death stare. His family helped peel us off the ground and Theodore scooted our asses straight back out the door.

Anthony, Theodore, Missy and I continued to go to Club Seventies on Sunday nights (cue *Blondie's* Heart of Glass.) It was the closest thing to Studio 54 that we had, and we couldn't stay away from something that marvelous. Lots of pulsating disco, loads of craziness and a river of drinks flowing. There was no Bianca Jagger on a white horse or a man in the moon with a cocaine spoon, but we took what we could get. We sat in the car drinking Zimas before getting out into the cold air and bouncing up to the big line in front of the building. A transsexual named Robin worked the door and let us in before all others because we were always in costume and really outrageous. We experimented with fashion a lot at that club, which was just glorious. Sometimes I would put individual lashes on the bottom of my eyes and pluck my eyebrows into nothing and wear straight hair parted down the middle to do a real Mod sort of look (which was so *not* seventies, but whatever). Other times I did this surfy theme with a shirt the color of an orange cream soda and some puca shells around my neck and white lipstick. I once wore Missy's grandma's house cap- it was full of white feathers and was meant to cover curlers I think. But I wore it with a black /white polka dotted sundress.

One night as we were about to walk in, a bunch of sweaty, nasty looking girls were leaving the club. I said, "If I am going to look like THAT when I come out, I don't even want to go IN." Right after I said it, I tripped and fell in front of everyone, in my feathered hat, while "Cutie Pie" thumped in the background.

We very often danced on the super high platforms in that club. Theodore wore his afro wig and bell bottoms and did lots of high kicks and shit. We always got more and more wild at that place as the night progressed, because the bartender had us tilt back our heads and open our mouths, and would pour straight vodka down our throats as often as we wanted. I recall that a) he had a crush on Missy and b) we were the only ones dressed up and entertaining the masses with our outrageousness- the club appeared to be paying us in booze.

Journal Entry 4/19/1994

Things seem to be pretty cool. I don't have to drive anyone around anywhere. I have my own space. I have the summer to look forward to. I am sitting outside of Cricca's Italian Deli on Topanga Canyon by my house, before school. I gained two pounds over the weekend because I stopped the diet pills I was taking. I have made more money at work being off of them, because I am not so irritable. I guess I should have known. I mean, wasn't this diet pill thing an episode on 90210 *or* Saved by the Bell *or something? Anyway, all the roommates had a big family dinner last night. They made scalloped potatoes, pasta, chicken breasts, and salad. I said grace, which everyone took seriously but Tim.*

This news is two weeks old, but the guy from Nirvana committed suicide. He was miserable and now everyone else is miserable. People are saying he was the voice of our generation. It is eerie to listen to my Nirvana CD now. I can't tell you how many times I have cried and cried to Nirvana songs in the past few years. I don't know what it was about Nirvana, but the strength of the songs, the angst of them- it is what a young person feels in their body when they are lonely, when they are sad, when they are disappointed, when they are scared. They made it into sounds instead of words. I appreciated that. I wasn't into the look of them and I didn't ever tell anyone I listened to them because I didn't want to be associated with Grunge- but I was a huge Nirvana fan, in secret. That music really carried me through some of the most horrible times of my life. The guy did us a service, providing that. Shame he is dead.

We had a huge Luau that May. I was used to huge parties and had the confidence to throw one. I ordered a bunch of Hawaiian decorations from a party supply place and all the roommates split the cost. Each of us invited everyone we ever knew, whether we liked them or not. We got four kegs of beer and put them out at the tiki bar by the pool. I invited all of the dancers I knew and told them to wear bikinis; I handed them grass skirts when they got there.

The guys from my work were always happy when I invited my Hollywood girlfriends over, as you can imagine. The girls would be frolicking in the pool, oblivious to creepy, mouth-breathing perverts in glasses watching them from a lawn chair in the dark.

Anyhow, the party was a huge rager. It got so big that some random guy stood at my front door and started charging people who were coming in, and he pocketed the money. A bunch of my old Hollywood friends came, and I just remember one of the musician guys pulling his dancer girlfriend across the front lawn by her hair, which was standard for an arguing Hollywood couple, but completely shocking to everyone else.

We were all sliding on the floor because it was a river of spilled drinks, and I faintly remember some guy from MTV's *The Real World* showing up. There were fights, skinny dipping, puking off balconies, cops at the door- you know, the standard events at a rager. I even jumped in the pool in my heavy platform shoes, which turned out to be very dangerous once I started sinking to the bottom and realized that they were like two bricks weighing me down. I had to try to unbuckle them off my ankles while drunk in the dark water- it was very Houdini.

I later bumped into a guy in my crowded backyard who I recognized as a snotty jock from my high school. He kind of looked me up and down and asked me what I was doing there, in a dickish fashion. I was like, *I **live** here. This is **my party**, bitch. And by the way, there is a cover charge...*

Five

CLOUD OF CRUSHED DREAMS

I turned twenty-one in September 1994, right when our lease was up on the Topanga house. The guys started clearing out their belongings, which were few. None of us really had anything. There were two fridges and one of them was so full of smelly rot inside, that when Tim opened it to get one last beer, he caught a whiff of it and jerked his beer bottle into his mouth and chipped his front tooth.

The kitchen had been piling up with stolen Pao Pao salad bowls and plates, crusted with rotten food. No one wanted to go in and pick through the mold and maggots to claim their plates and cups and things. Everyone just left their kitchen stuff there and moved out. Anthony went in one day and cleaned everything with a clothespin on his nose. He packed up all of the stuff and kept it. I still have some of the mixing bowls to this day.

Everyone went their separate ways. Blake moved in with a friend and Tim and Lucas moved out together from what I remember. Sadly, Shaun Peterson died two years later, doing a stunt on a TV show. I wished I would have told him how much I appreciated his help instead of being such an asshole at that time. Shaun wasn't the only one to die-three other people who hung out at the Topanga house with us actually died in different ways within the following five years. *Young* people. It messed with my head for a while. I didn't understand why people were dropping like flies.

I clung to Anthony and begged him to let me move in with him somewhere. He was game. He told me to find the place, check it out, and he would put down the deposit. I found an apartment a few doors down from Missy in Sherman Oaks. I liked that it was that close to her. I didn't realize just how ugly the building was though. I hadn't inspected many apartment buildings at that time; well actually, I had inspected *zero* apartment buildings, so I just said yes to it because it was cheap. The tenant who was showing me the place said it was $750 a month for a two bedroom, one bath. The living room had some hateful wood paneling across an entire wall and very thin doors that you could kick a hole through very easily (I foresaw that it was likely that one of us would be doing so.) It was kind of set up like a motel, because there were no security gates, you could just walk up to the front door from a stairway that opened out onto a public driveway. So that didn't feel too safe, but nothing ever did.

Anyway, I saw the place and thought it was good enough, so we had to go meet with the landlord so he could run our credit. Anthony was nervous about his recent car repossession and I *had* no credit. We starting plotting.

"Okay," said Anthony, "If he is straight, you flirt with him. If he is gay, I will flirt with him. Got it?"

A thin, limp-wristed man with droopy, brilliant blue eyes answered the door with a little dog in a sweater yapping behind him. "**San**dy! Sh**ush**!" he said. I looked at Anthony as if to say *All yours.* We came in the house and the dog started sniffing us. "Oh, he *likes* you," said the landlord, as he led us to the kitchen table. He offered us some Valium for having had to "deal with that traffic on the way over." We gladly popped the pills as if it were completely normal. Then he went and put on the soundtrack to *Sunset Boulevard.* I lifted an eyebrow at Anthony as if to say *Now there is no question.* Henry sat down and stared at us.

"I ran your credit," he said to Anthony. There was silence. Anthony started to shift in his seat. Henry was just staring at him. Anthony started to spill.

"Well, I recently got that repo on my credit, but it is all figured out now."

Henry nodded and said nothing. He just kept staring at Anthony. Anthony continued digging himself in a hole, out of being nervous.

"And I may have had a few late charges here and there, but that was because I was trying to get some decent furniture if you know what I mean."

Henry nodded. There was more silence. Suddenly, he spoke.

"Have you seen *Sunset Boulevard*?"

I said no and Anthony said yes at the same time. Anthony kicked me under the table. Then Henry narrowed his eyes at Anthony and said,

"Do I *know* you from somewhere?"

I kicked Anthony back, harder. Anthony fidgeted.

"Ah, no. No, I don't think so."

Henry spoke right over him: "Where did you live two years ago?"

Anthony stuttered that he had lived in Burbank, but Henry wasn't listening.

"You lived off Santa Monica in West Hollywood. Yes. I think I *do* know you."

Anthony realized that he had hooked up with our future landlord right about then. I was hoping it wasn't the guy who paid him with a bucket of chicken. The landlord then told us that his dog liked us, so we could have the place. We looked at each other.

Henry said, "If Sandy likes you, *I* like you."

We moved into our apartment the next weekend. It was a block south of Ventura Boulevard, where the 405 and 101 freeways meet. The neighborhood was a mix of crappy old apartments and some semi-new ones. The street was lined with parked cars and appeared to be some sort of a shortcut. Cars were zipping by all hours of the day and night. It was the location of the next phase of my life.

The inhabitants of Sherman Oaks were the young people who, again, had moved from other states to make it big in Los Angeles, but who couldn't afford to live somewhere nice. It was a very busy town: close to Studio City, close to Billy Blanx Tae Bo classes and Pink Cheeks skin care salon. There was a large selection of struggling actors and actresses; waiters, adult film stars and dancers. It was a lot of people without their families. People who were out on their own, struggling. It was not a happy community. It was like the land of the lost toys. I think a lot of the people, especially the girls, were kind of down because they may have come out to L.A. to get into acting, but finding that they were not getting parts, had to pay their rent somehow. And that 'somehow,' more often than not, involved stripping or adult films.

Anthony often bought porn magazines, all types. He came tearing through the door one day with a picture of our neighbors in *Hustler*. They were a young, hot couple from the Midwest who apparently did a pictorial together. Jenna Jameson, who wasn't super famous yet, lived a few blocks down. A famous adult star now known as Dale DaBone, was a waiter at Pao Pao when I worked there (sometime between 1994 and 1996- I don't remember the year.) Not that those people can't be happy- I am sure they are. But the area in which I lived just kind of reeked of sadness to me. It was this cloud of crushed dreams.

Just as I was relieved when I left the British folk, I was terribly relieved to be away from the Topanga house. I had started to fall for Blake and I knew I needed to get away from him. I still had to work with him, and it was distracting me to the point of wanting to quit my job. There is nothing worse than being a server alongside another server you have hooked up with and still have feelings for, because the job consisted of a lot of flirting. He was constantly flirting with chicks and ignoring me and it was like a stab in my heart. I tried to flirt as much as possible too, but I was crestfallen and couldn't do a good job of it. So, my problem was not just that I was heartbroken over the lack of attention from this guy I fell for, but it was also that I couldn't concentrate on making my own money. If something stopped me from being happy and lively, my tips suffered. My ability to *survive* suffered. I had to think of something fast. I had to get rid of him. And that is exactly what I did.

Birdie came over to my apartment one night, got really stoned or pilled out or something, and slept over. Blake was partying with us that night and slept over as well, just so he could try and hook up with her. He was not successful in doing so, but he somehow thought that if he stayed there with her while I went to work the next day, he could score. I don't know if I have ever been so jealous. He was supposed to work with me that day, but he called in sick.

It sounds like a total lie, but this is really what happened and I am not even kidding: I went to work and played on the insecurity of my boss, Grant. I said, "Blake is lying. He isn't even sick. He is at my house right now, sleeping. Are you going to keep letting him get *away* with that? I thought you were our *boss*." He was like, "I am," and I sort of taunted him, saying, "You never *fire* anyone. He always does this and you never make that move- I thought you had power." I am NOT kidding; it was so ridiculous the things I was saying. Even more ridiculous was the fact that he was totally falling for these stupid clichéd lines! So he says, "I will fire him right now," and I was like, "No you won't; you never fire *anyone*." Low and behold, he fired Blake! Just like that. Gone. I no longer had to worry about working with him. I was so overjoyed! The revenge was so sweet; I smiled for a week straight.

It was the beginning of a new era. A time when all of the right players come together and make magic, as only restaurant crews can understand (okay...maybe magic is a little strong of a word- let's just say really, really fun.) It was the fall of 1994. A new guy was hired to replace Blake. His name was Jack. He was a Latino with bleached white hair and a baritone voice that sounded like an announcer. He had a vocabulary that was so advanced, he left most people scratching their heads. He was not only well-spoken, but he had a quick wit and was quite cultured. I suspected he was gay- and I don't know exactly why I thought it, but I did. I guess it was when he told me about an Yves St. Laurent (in the correct pronunciation) scarf he wore to a family dinner. I was like, *okay, girlfriend ain't straight.* He tried telling me about his Asian girlfriend and I just looked at him like, *bitch please.* Jack was a little stuffy at first, but I could see that he would be fun once he let loose at little.

I walked in one day shortly thereafter to see another new hire. This time it was a girl named Allison Rogers. She was a classically pretty girl with long brown hair that had a red tint to it. She didn't need to wear much makeup, she was natural and clean looking. She looked a lot like an olive-skinned Natalie Wood, whom I always adored, but a

Natalie Wood who could fight. Real cute, with sort of a tough edge. It seemed like she would fuck me up if I crossed her. I sensed the toughness about her by the way she carried her keys in her back pocket. I stared at those keys for a couple of shifts. She was in the Pao Pao uniform, so I couldn't get any clues off of her style or wardrobe, the typical way one would read another person. All I had were those keys. The key chain was wrapped with duct tape and there was a bottle opener alongside it. Okay. She was a guy's girl, a beer drinker. Probably mellow, low key. She didn't talk much, so I didn't know what to make of her. I thought for sure she would hate me because she was not friendly toward me and made no move to be social with me. I didn't know if I could crack her- there was always a certain type of girl who just couldn't stand obnoxious people like me.

One day Michael Jackson's "Don't Stop till you Get Enough" was playing. Jack and I were sitting in the take out area, and I did an imitation of the song. Allison heard me and laughed so hard she almost shattered the glass wall next to us. I felt good that she thought I was funny. She warmed to me a lot that day, and kind of listened to Jack and me for entertainment purposes. Allison was slow to reveal herself. She preferred to sit back and watch the craziness, so I still wasn't sure if we would get any closer.

One night soon thereafter, I had a party at my apartment. I invited everyone from work and insisted Jack and Allison come. I thrusted some strong drinks into their hands and slurred at them to join in on the game I had created: I had a Twister mat on the floor and decided to combine it with truth or dare for the ultimate drinking game. They were good sports about it (If I recall correctly, Allison got to see one of our cute co-workers' balls.)

By the end of the night, Jack was crawling on the ground, laughing, with a pink frozen drink in his hand. Anthony loved him. Once they started clubbing together, Jack felt more comfortable about admitting he was gay. He was not interested in Anthony romantically, but he loved going out with him because it was fun. Anthony and I started to joke that we were a professional service that yanked people out of the closet.

We all started to go out together. One night, we proceeded to get shit-faced drunk and get into Anthony's car with our beers. Anthony drove us toward four pylons in the street and screeched to a halt when he realized he was about to crash into them. He decided he wanted to go around them. He pulled up onto the sidewalk and crashed through someone's potted plants. Right when he drove off the curb into the street on the other side, a cop's light flashed and a siren made one "Wh-ew" sound. We all giggled. The cop walked up to Anthony and saw all of us in the back with beers. No one wore seatbelts and some of us were sitting on other's laps. Anthony's headlight was out and there were a million other things wrong with the clunker he was driving. The cop sighed and shook his head, probably thinking that it would take the whole night to list all of the shit wrong with the situation. There could not have been enough room on a ticket. He told us to go home and left.

Another night, I went out with Jack, Anthony and a nice girl from work. One of the guys was invited to some crazy porn party up in the hills and we wanted to see what it was all about. We picked up some booze and headed up Coldwater Canyon (or was it down?), singing along to the radio. We got out of the car at some place that was overlooking a cliff and started walking up toward the doors that had loud music pulsating through them. Jack and the girl cracked their beers and started to bring them to their lips and we heard "Freeze! Police."

Some plain clothes cop came over, showed a badge, and wrote Jack a ticket for drinking in public. He ran the nice girl's ID and it turned out she had unpaid speeding tickets that had turned into warrants, so he handcuffed her and brought her to his police car which was hidden around the corner or something. He came back to us and told us he had to take her to jail! There were full on orgies and debauchery going on inside the party, but we were the ones who were getting in trouble! We all left the driveway of the party and went out dancing somewhere, completely ignoring the fact that our friend was in jail. I recall getting home that night and watching Anthony take his canary, Peeps, out of her cage and trying to put her in his mouth. He got her in at one point and her legs were sticking out- it was so sad. She flew out and almost got killed in the ceiling fan. We caught her and put her back into her cage, which had a miniature disco ball inside. I put a bunch of Barbie furniture in there: a dressing table, a chair, a phone, and some other stuff. It ended up getting all full of poo.

***

Something kept bothering me. It was this *voice*. You would think it was the voice of reason, but it wasn't. It was the sound of Blake's voice. *Blue collar. White trash. Split ends. No manicure.* I started to worry. I thought *if I don't look good, who will want to take care of me? I will be screwed.* I was barely getting by on being semi-pretty and fun; people were amused by me and kind of took care of me. I knew that the worse I looked, the less likely I would have that luxury.

Anthony was taking care of me at that point, and it was only because I walked around in skimpy clothes and attracted guys for him to try and sway. And I was trying to pull that off looking like a total heifer. How long could it last? I wasn't sure. I had to think about the future. I saw no value in myself whatsoever besides the possibility of being beautiful. I thought my looks would be my ticket to security. What else did I have to offer? I couldn't think of one single skill or talent or interest I had. Those thoughts were for kids in college who could choose what they wanted to do and their parents would pay for the schooling. That wasn't the way it worked for kids like me. This wasn't some fun little game where I could sit around dreaming of a career. I would literally be on the street if someone weren't always helping me out.

I had to fix things, and fix them fast. I once went from a nerd to a Hollywood Babe. Could I go from a puffy, trashed loser who put parking cones on her head to a beautifully groomed, feminine bombshell? I didn't quite know the rules of Encino or Sherman Oaks or wherever the hell I was. I knew that even if I studied them and was ready to implement them, I would need money to pull it off and I had none. It was going to be next to impossible to change my image.

But that never stopped me before.

Six

THE CLIQUE

I went into public relations mode. The first thing that needed to happen was that I needed to slim down. It was completely unacceptable to be overweight in Los Angeles. Period. There was no way around it. It was a sign of laziness and lack of dedication to your looks, neither of which would be permitted. If you couldn't afford to go to the gym, you needed to go running or find some other way. No excuses.

In L.A., the gym was more important than church is to most people. It is where images were made and maintained, bodies were sculpted, abs were flattened, and asses were tightened. Egos were pumped, confidence was gained. When people in L.A. can't get to the gym, they get very moody and cranky.

I started going without food and exercising five nights a

week, dripping with sweat while running up in the hills behind my apartment. One time a horrible rape was reported a few blocks from my house. It had occurred on my exercise route. I thought about not going out running at night, but then I thought of my fat ass and decided to risk it. I felt desperate to be thin. It became the most important thing in my life, above all else. If I ate too much, I simply induced vomiting, just as I had done in my junior high days. I spent a lot of time bent over a toilet seat with my finger down my throat. I also started taking laxatives. The idea of getting the food out of my body immediately appealed to me. I didn't want anything sitting in my stomach.

It only took me a few months to slim down with the methods I was using, but I had to pay a price. I had to hide vomit-stained fingers, watery eyes and eroded teeth. A few times the food got stuck in a clump in my throat and I nearly choked to death. The blood vessels broke in my eyes.

The laxatives were no better. Sometimes I was in the middle of a conversation with a guy at work and would have to run to the bathroom so I didn't crap my pants. I could go on for another four pages about the torture I went through in order to slim down, but let's move on.

I had tackled the hardest part: weight. Next, I knew I had to figure out the grooming aspect. I started with the nails. I started getting manicures at some Korean place where they said "you pick cuh-law" as a greeting. Many times they would do a shitty job, for instance, cut the hell out of my cuticles until they were bleeding, or make the acrylic nails way too thick. I would try to yell at them and they would conveniently forget English.

There was a salon called Allen Edwards that was next door
to Pao Pao. For those of you who don't know who Allen
Edwards is, he is the guy who created Farrah Fawcett's
famous signature cut. He also did the hair of Suzanne
Somers, Raquel Welch, and more recently Renee
Zellweger and Julianne Moore. So anyway, this famous
salon was right next door to my work. The stylists,
colorists, waxers and assistants all came in for lunch. It
was absolute insanity how beautiful the staff was. I tried
not to stare at them. I made friends with one of the gay
colorists and he told me to come get my hair cut and
highlighted…for *free*. Uh…*yes please.*

Then I started tanning. My skin was already olive and
usually tan, but I felt I needed to be tanner so my blue eyes
would stand out. I closed myself into the big old sandwich
of lights, sweating my balls off in the bright purple glow. I
wore my little goggles and listened to *92.3 The Beat Jams*,
hoping I didn't catch some sort of cooties from the sweat
of some porn star who used the bed before me.

I was broke, SO broke after the manicures and tanning, but
I considered them an investment and was sure I would
make the money back in tips. Sure enough, my tips
increased. I used that money for new clothes.

I decided very deliberately that I would have a preppy,
school girl, baby-doll type of look. I got the idea from a
Patrick DeMarchelier shoot from some magazine. It felt
clean, feminine and pretty and I thought the pastels would
look good against the dark tan and dark hair. I wore baby
pink, powder blue, sugary lilac, soft yellow and pale mint

green. I wore my false eyelashes and some sheer, sparkly, vanilla-scented lip gloss. It sounds completely preposterous now, but the look was a hit back then for some odd reason. It was different than all of the black everyone else in L.A. was wearing. I stood out.

I kind of snapped back into that vixen mode I once knew. When I walked into a room, I held my head up and worked that shit. People turned and looked, just because I looked so different. If you are going to wear something that could be laughed at, you need to have a ton of confidence to convince the onlookers that you are cool and they are mere laypeople. Inside, I felt obnoxious, but I made myself walk the walk.

The third thing I knew I had to do was align myself with other beautiful women. I was not one of those girls who wanted to be the prettiest girl in her group. My value would surely decrease if I was in a group of sloppy hags, no matter what I looked like. I started hanging out with the prettiest girls I knew: my Hollywood girlfriends, who had also distanced themselves from our former crowd. The pretty clique was Missy, two other girls named Lisel and Poppy, and of course Birdie.

Missy (her last name was O'Malley) looked kind of like Molly Sims, with lighter blonde hair and a deeper tan. She had insane measurements and was a fucking knockout-men would trip, fall, and crash their cars looking at her. I had never seen so many guys turn into idiots! She had these big sparkly doe eyes and a huge smile that showed all of her perfect white teeth. She wore pale, cotton-candy pink lipstick, and black 1960's eyeliner. She was really bubbly and happy; really fun. And of course she was also very comforting, like a blankie. I always felt good around her, like everything was going to be okay. She was sweet and romantic and always had a good heart- you could feel it when you were around her.

Lisel Stevenson was a co-worker and friend of Missy's. She looked like a blond version of Stephanie Seymour, circa the "November Rain" video: long legs, gorgeous face and ice blue eyes. She was very matter-of-fact and did not take any shit. She was also a crack up. She would get so wild at parties I thought I would pee my pants laughing at her. She would always be the first to skinny dip but she would also be the first to defend her friends against any wrongdoing or injustice. She was really a mother hen. People always listened to her, because even though she was a dancer, she could speak properly and could talk her way in and out of things with intelligence. She had that bitchy Encino woman's voice that sent back food at restaurants and demanded refunds on things. People automatically backed down to her. I always felt safe around her.

Poppy Holloway had super long, pin-straight, apricot colored hair; apple green eyes and huge silicone boobs on a very slender frame. Her face looked sort of like Denise Richards. She was sweet and almost childlike, sort of Marilyn Monroe-ish in demeanor. She had already had lots of plastic surgery at twenty-four years old, and rumor was that she paid for none of it herself. She was secretive about her job. I figured she was somehow involved in the adult entertainment industry, but she said she was a model. She had a twin sister who was an actress. Poppy was relatively shy and a total homebody, despite her line of work. She often became very paranoid and would drive herself crazy with worry over something very minor. She could also scam the pants off any man in her line of sight. She was a pro.

All of us were into drinking vodka, dancing, laughing, and gossiping. Again, our former scene was officially over, so we girls migrated to the next party stop: The L.A. Clubs.

My friends were the perfect patrons for these clubs, because they were above average in looks and in measurements. Boob jobs and hair extensions were not commonplace among the public at that point, but the dancers and models had the long hair extensions, the blondest hair, the biggest boobs, the brightest and flashiest clothes, and the biggest smiles. It was their *profession* to outdo the other women in the room, by any means possible. I operated the same way. It was all about standing out in a crowd.

The reason to be so overly done-up to go to a nightclub in L.A. was simple: if you didn't look good, you couldn't come in.

You couldn't just *pay* and get in- you had to be chosen by the doormen. It might be that way everywhere, I don't know. I just know that in L.A., there was no guarantee that you were welcome inside the doors of an establishment. It was no secret: good looks and good bodies were the only way in. I don't know how it worked with guys. I noticed that certain guys could pay off the doormen and get in. As far as girls went, if they were overweight or not attractive, they were shit out of luck. They simply had to leave.

There was always a crowd around the velvet ropes; people

who were just standing there feeling more and more crappy about themselves. People that felt good when they left the house but were slowly getting depressed thinking about why they weren't let in. They were thinking that they should have worked out more, gotten more plastic surgery, dieted more. You could see their faces dropping, their inner voices arguing with them to just leave, to stop being subjected to the cruelty; but they would stay and fight the voice, thinking that maybe the doorman didn't see them, thinking that maybe if they waited a little longer they would be let in...

So anyway, there I was, in the midst of all of this club stuff. I was newly twenty-one, but I had been going to clubs since I was sixteen, so none of the politics were anything new to me. I knew how it worked.

I was pleased with myself for pulling myself together, and was enjoying being in a group of girls that made jaws drop. I felt like things went into slow motion when we walked into rooms. I somehow knew that I wouldn't always have it like that, so I really enjoyed those moments.

Journal Entry 12/25/1994

I just spent Christmas day with Missy at a beach house in Malibu. I don't know what my family was doing. My sister and I used to get so excited for Christmas Eve at my grandparents. There was always a big dinner and lots of decorations. There was only one lamp on, of course, because the house had to be as dark as a cave. I remember the silver tree with red ornaments and lots of gifts wrapped in groovy seventies geographical designs. I can still see that wrapping paper: silver paper with neon pink print and turquoise blue trim and red paper with lime green, lemon yellow, cobalt blue and metallic gold designs. Aunt Billie's dog Skipper would tear open his own presents and shred wrapping paper everywhere. There was always a wooden bowl of nuts on the coffee table: Brazil nuts, hazelnuts and almonds along with a metal nutcracker. There was a glorious nativity scene on top of the mantle with bejeweled wise men and baby lambs encrusted with tiny pearls. Mary, Joseph, and baby Jesus were all drowned in sparkle. There were three little heavy red and green bells that sat under the fireplace that said "Joy," "Noel," and "Peace;" One was long and thin, one fat and rounded and one a perfect bell shape.

Being in school used to add to the Christmas spirit. We always made a craft of some sort, like a wreath of gold spray-painted tree pods or a paper Christmas tree. Each class sang a Christmas carol in the school show. You would always come home for Christmas vacation with an armful of crafts and candy canes and Santa Clauses with cotton ball beards, or a reindeer made out of the shape of your traced hand. My mother used to put up a little snowy town on top of her upright piano. There was a big sheet of cotton snow and little houses that we would light up with tiny tree lights. Our cat Max used to jump up there. She would be very delicate with her paws when she walked over all of the houses, so she wouldn't mess anything up and then would somehow lower her body into the snow. She thought the whole thing was for her and looked very regal.

Okay, so, I went to the El Rey the other night and was dancing on the stage to Notorious B.I.G.'s "Juicy." The next thing I knew, that super-hot guy from General

Hospital *was dancing with me. I was like, whoa- no way. We were dancing to the side of the stage, with my back toward some curtains. He started being all sexy and was kind of backing me up, so I tried to be all cute and was dancing backwards, trying to feel for the wall. My back hit the curtains, but I felt no wall. The next thing I knew, there was a big poof of curtains flapping, and I saw my feet up in the air. I saw his head looking down at me in shock. It got smaller and smaller as I fell backwards into the dark. By the time I untangled myself out of the wings of the side stage, he was gone.*

Journal Entry 12/28/1994

*I went to some wrap party with Anthony the other night. He always wants me to be a total bimbo. It made me feel like shit last time. I realized people were laughing **at** me, not with me. I am a game for him. He doesn't really care about me, but he is the person closest to me in my life right now. He is the person taking care of me. He doesn't judge me, even knowing every bad thing that I've done or do. He isn't one to judge, because he does whatever HE wants, no matter how hedonistic. He says he has been not only around the block, but "into neighboring cities."*

Anthony and Missy get along fabulously. They both make lots of cash and spend lots of cash and they both keep things real light. They don't want to think about the problems of life. They really keep my spirits up most of the time- I am not a big laugher, but I laugh around them quite a bit, and that feels good.

Birdie passed on going to Europe for the Heidi Fleiss people, but she is still in contact with them. She said she is doing some sort of voiceover work for now, after she 'blew it' with Charlie Sheen one night. She said they had her go out and eat at a fancy restaurant to see how her table manners were (hers are excellent), but she 'wasn't quite right.' I wonder if that just meant she didn't put out. She doesn't do things she doesn't want to do, I will give her that.

Journal Entry 1/2/1995

Anthony and I are cleaning for our dinner party tonight. It keeps accidentally expanding larger. Our kitten is sitting here staring at me. His name is Patrick, after a serial killer in some book Anthony just read. I didn't necessarily want the kitten named after him, but our pushy neighbor from downstairs convinced Anthony it was a great idea. We always humor him and feel bad for him for being such a loser with no friends. (sigh.) I miss Lestat, who we lost at the other house to the coyotes in the hills.

I have realized that I am getting shallower. I can only think stupid, vapid thoughts, and here they are:

1) I am glad I didn't spend that $50 on those stilettos from Frederick's of Hollywood for New Year's Eve because I never would've worn them again (I wore a metallic gold dress.)

2) My face is getting fatter; I need to get some anti-bloating pills to suck out the water.

3) I need to jog tomorrow or I won't get the time of day from any guy.

4) Wesley is cute and I am embarrassed that I was so trashed in front of him at Club Seventies (I knocked him right in the teeth with my skull.)

Wesley was a new guy that started working at Pao Pao. I ain't gonna lie- he was hot. He was a nineteen-year-old baseball player with tan skin, dark hair, and green eyes. He was tall and had a low voice. He was also a big stoner. He was one of those guys that is so stoned that they just laugh at nothing and say *Whoa* a lot. Courtney Salzberg beat me to him and "hung out" with him almost immediately following his hire. She quickly reported to me that he had a son, hoping that I would be turned off and would back off. I was like, *bitch please; I was dating guys wearing garter belts with pet ferrets locked in their bathroom.* My standards were low enough to skim the sidewalk.

One night I pointed out Wesley to Anthony, and he was licking his chops. He said I had to get him over to the apartment so we could get him drunk. Jack thought he was too stupid to be attractive, but he was all for the train wreck unfolding. We were prepared to be highly entertained. So I invited him over to have some drinks; lemon drops to be exact. After a while, we started taking shots of water and let him keep drinking vodka. After telling us his mother told him he had bedroom eyes, he took one of the lemons we were using to chase the vodka with and wanted to show us his pitching arm. He threw a fastball lemon at our couch a few times. Then he must've been off, because he threw the next lemon right through the living room window. Glass shattered all over the couch and the whole window was gone. I wanted to laugh, but I was so pissed. I yelled at him and gave him a broom and ordered him outside to clean the glass. We watched from the upstairs window as he swept up the glass from the driveway, slurring and laughing to himself. Anthony looked at me and said, "Damn girl. He is *dumb*. Hot and dumb." I was planning to hook up with him, but he had ruined the moment and I couldn't act like I was okay with him shattering my window.

Wesley admitted a few days later that he not only had a son, but was 'friends' with a psychotic girl who paid for all of his clothes and his rent. *Okay,* I thought, *so you're like a musician. This is my forte.* The girl was obsessed with him in a sad way (well, I guess there is nothing *happy* about obsession.) Anthony and I witnessed this when we took Wesley to Club Seventies one night. The girl saw the love of her life with me and burst into tears. He felt bad for her and went to console her. I felt bad for her too. I thought, *eh, I know how it feels. I will let him go over there and say what he has to say.* I sipped my drink. After a little while I realized that the motherfucker was spending *way* too much time consoling. I marched over to them and announced "time is **UP**," then I dragged him away from her crying eyes and broken heart. Hey, I was nice, but I was not *that* nice.

Just when I thought Wesley's lemon throwing incident was the dumbest thing I had seen him do, he decided to do something even more stupid. I gave him a ride to work one day (of course he had no car) and he shoved his baseball team health exam papers in my glove compartment while we went through the Burger King drive-thru on Ventura Boulevard (I had to pay for both of us.) I dropped him off at work and drove back home, pulling out the papers to snoop on his ass. I nearly choked on my chicken sandwich when I read that he had had an extreme case of genital warts. They were so bad that he had to have some surgery on his thingie. *Great*. And just because it still cracks me up, I have to mention that one day when I left him at my apartment while I went to work, my neighbor from downstairs came up and said that Wesley was doing jumping jacks by himself in my room. The neighbor said he just kept hearing this huge BOOM! On the floor and he couldn't figure it out. Then he listened very closely and heard a little "clap" after each boom. Dude, I know. I *know*.

1/ 2/ 1995 continued

Anthony is still cleaning and I am in no way lending a hand. He is also cooking everyone dinner, including my friends. I didn't just knock Wesley in the teeth last night; I also did some other stupid things. I was hanging out with my Transsexual friend Robin and I was knocking people over on the dance floor while doing my disco spins. I hit my face on the wall after trying to tell Wesley off. I was taking people's drinks when they set them down, and drinking them myself. I was spraying my friend's names on the wall outside with mace. Then I went home (after being really, really mean to various men) and made pasta. Anthony threw his keys in the fish bowl and then we made this really rude, slurring outgoing message on the answering machine: "This is a no-nonsense house, so if you have a problem, you can get the fuck out. We don't have time for fuckin problems around here. Everyone really sucks," etc. The phone is ringing off the hook right now.

Journal Entry 1/3/1995

*P.J. looked at Wesley taking the lonnnng way to the back door while carrying a heavy tray of food and said, "All good-looking guys are either gay or dumb." One of the girls looked at him and said, "Well then what does that make **you**?"*

*Life is no different today except that I am now on the diet the rest of L.A. is on: fresh spinach, brown rice, and water. My new boss asked me if I were modeling and how my "actressing" was going (huh?). My old boss, who is still here, came up and sniffed me really hard and said that I smelled great and that his wife wasn't giving him sex so he was on edge (shudders). An old co-worker who was recently fired came in and asked me out. I said no. The hostess came over and said she was hanging out with an Elite model who I'd love. She said, and I quote, "She is really vain and shallow- you'd **love** her. She talks about eyelashes and all that stuff." Can you **believe** that? I was insulted at that one, of all the shit tonight. I mean, geez, I was talking to her a few days ago about how you try so hard on New Year's Eve to look better than you did all year, that you end up looking worse. It backfires. I told her how I dropped my one pair of false lashes in the glue and how neither I nor my friends could walk in the shoes we were wearing...I guess I came off as vain and shallow.*

A different co-worker told me last night that I have a great act at work. He says I project an image people want and that people think I am dumber than I really am. I didn't know what to say to that. I do know what I am projecting and I do market myself to my advantage- I have to do it. People take short cuts. I depend on these tips at this restaurant to make a living.

The only problem with doing so much pretending, is that it's hard to develop, hard to progress. I am getting further and further from who I want to be. I am trying to think of good qualities I have, but there aren't many. Well, there is one I can think of. I don't lie often. Also, I defend people who can't defend themselves. But that is just because I like getting into arguments I think.

*One thing that **isn't** good is that I turn on my friends a lot quicker than I used to. I don't return phone calls. I gossip horribly. I give away people's secrets because I forget which are private. That is an abominable quality. It really hits the spot when I gossip to people. I seek revenge on people who have hurt me, at any cost. I am lazy...this will go on forever. I don't think I am a nice person. I have humiliated countless people (most of whom deserved it, but still). Sometimes I am very cold and evil. It makes me sad. I need to be stopped. I need to get back to the roots of the person I used to be. I don't remember the happiness my heart used to hold. It was really simple and I can't find it. Before all of the trauma of my crazy life happened, I was a wonderful girl. I am embarrassed of what I have become.*

Seven

FEEL THE EMPTINESS

Journal Entry 1/4/1995

Wesley wasn't so sexy today when he plopped his wisdom tooth down on the counter when I was doing paperwork. He needs supervision. I can't mother him like he needs. John tried to ask me out for a drink, I said no. David bossed me around and I let him (nice pecs). One of the cooks tried to ask me to be his girlfriend in Chinese. Basically, it wasn't a great night because I only made nine dollars. I came home, ate a meatball sub from Subway, and for the rest of the night did waist and bust exercises.

Journal Entry 1/7/1995

Last night sucked. This guy was making fun of Poppy and me behind our backs at the Rainbow (she dragged me there, okay?) Missy saw, and told us. I confronted the guy, who was with his date. I asked him why he was talking shit. He told me to fuck off and that he didn't care what I thought. I said, "Just... 'fuck off'? You don't even **know** me and you just randomly tell me to fuck off? You're just...ruining my **night**?" I didn't get it. He just laughed in my face. It was this really out of style guy with long, permed hair. I tried reasoning with the guy because it was really bothering me. He said "fuck you" again, with a smirk. I snapped. I threw my drink, glass and all, straight into his face with force. His head was soaked and the straw was stuck in his perm. I said, "No, fuck **you**," and walked away.

Journal Entry 1/15/1995

I got staggering drunk with Birdie last night, who wore a furry, cartoon pink dress that was made out of stuffed animal fur or something. When I got home, I was locked out of my apartment. I passed out in my downstairs neighbor's bed and peed my pants while I was sleeping! He was washing his sheets today in the laundry room and didn't mention it. How embarrassing.

Anthony invited a bunch of strangers over from the club. I don't approve of this shit. He just popped his head in here (its 2 a.m.) and is slurring that Jack is bringing back these hot guys who they want really badly. Then he tried to butter me up and said I was beautiful. I said, "Just shut the fuck up, don't fuckin' **lie**," and shut my door on him. Oh my gosh, now I hear girls' voices. I want to go out there and get my contact lens case out of the bathroom, but there is some random guy in there. I feel like I want to move out. I have a feeling I am not going to like Jack much after tonight. I work with him and all, and we have fun, but he *gets Anthony into too much trouble and then just waltzes home to his parent's house to leave us with the trail of bodies behind him.*

I hung out with Poppy the other day, who had just come back from a pool party with Corey Feldman of all people. She was obsessing on her nose job. She was making me look at before and after pictures of her. I had to tell her it was perfect three times! She thinks it is too wide. I said it had only been three weeks, what did she expect?

I am sad lately. I am not evolving. And I am sick of people asking me what I am going to do with my life, because I **don't know.** *I don't have an answer. I was so promising when I was younger, so ambitious. But things have changed. I can't go back to my true self. Maybe I never want to again. It only makes me want to cry. Even if I were to return to my original interests and hobbies and thoughts, my family has disbanded. The surroundings have vanished. I guess they do for everyone. Especially around here. No one has family around here.*

My dad wrote me a letter after Christmas. He used to be a good father, but then he kind of just went crazy. He got heavily into drugs. I am so sick of thinking about how he betrayed me. My mom calls every once and a while. She is different now. She is hard and cold compared to naïve and sweet. When I was a kid, I felt a real sense of security being in a warm happy home with a mother who was there for me when I returned home from school. She used to make homemade bread- it was the best smell in the world. She let the dough rise in the hallway for some reason, covered with a dishtowel. She also made great birthday cakes; she was really into cake decorating and had all these neat pans and supplies. She always had hobbies and projects going. She was into candy making, stained glass, making candles and doing needlepoint. She even got patterns and made us dresses. She was very artistic.

She kept a lot of art and craft and supplies around, in case my sister or I wanted to make something: construction paper, glue, crayons, markers, Play-Doh, yarn, whatever. One time I made a doll out of paper/ toilet paper/ paper towels. I rolled up a head, drew a cute face on it, and then glued on some yarn hair. Then I taped on a torso, legs and arms. And I didn't just stop at one, I made like, four or five of them. We always had the supplies to make anything our brain could think up. And I don't recall ever having to share many supplies, if any, because my sister didn't have the urge to make five dolls out of toilet paper like I did. She only had the urge to eat five pieces of Laughing Cow cheese and watch five cartoons. I would do something like construct an entire space ship out of construction paper, complete with planets and neighboring galaxies, while she inspected the inside of her eyelids and agreed to let me size her for a costume I was gluing together out of candy wrappers or something crazy like that. I had a big imagination and was relentless in my visions. I built sets for plays, carnivals and shit, I even made The Price is Right *game show out of all of those art supplies. I tape-recorded myself saying "Come on down! You're the next contestant on the Price is Right!" I forced my sister to run through the den to bid on some Windex and SOS pads and she had no idea what they cost. Nor did I. But it didn't matter because she was the only contestant, so I pulled her ass into the showcase showdown and let her win the trip to Costa Rica, the pool table and the Winnebago. I probably yelled at her for not showing enough enthusiasm at winning the grand prize.*

If we were painting, playing office, school, whatever it was, she couldn't quite live up to what I considered acceptable. She would often kind of let me down due to her sheer laziness and lack of zest- she was not interested in perfection or excellence. I had to push her to meet my criteria. I always had a vision that she didn't share, but she was having fun so she played along. She knew it meant a lot to me.

One time she wrote my name on the wall under a light switch, to try to get me in trouble. I remember looking at my name on the wall and thinking two things: One, that it was very clear it wasn't me that wrote it, because I did not write in a downward diagonal fashion and with each letter a different size, and second, I thought: Wow. She is pretty brave. I remember thinking it wasn't like her to do something like that to get me in trouble, I kind of admired it.

My sister wants nothing to do with me now. It hurts me that she keeps such a distance from me, but she doesn't have to keep in touch if she doesn't want to. She is going through a general outcast stage and the last person she wants to be around is someone like me. She despises people like me. She is the main person who tells me I am different now. She used to really admire me a lot, but now she doesn't like what I am about. She said she is worried about it. She should worry about getting off drugs, not about me.

Eventually, people lose touch with themselves. I can't very well remain a ten year old in glasses; writing plays and reading stacks of books and dreaming of running a business. I have bills to pay and minimal skills that will allow me to pay them. I am in L.A. and the currency here is looks, which allow me things like free food, free drinks/entertainment, getting out of tickets, getting my car fixed- those sorts of things. My looks are insurance- insurance that someone will help me if I really need it. If you are fat and ugly and standing in the rain with a flat tire, no one around here would stop. I need to be on point, because I am alone. All I can say is that it is next to impossible for me to be healthy and happy. I am in survival mode. Health and especially happiness are afterthoughts; luxuries.

Journal Entry 2/7/1995

Wesley got fired and I haven't seen him. I heard he has a restraining order against him for beating up a girlfriend and he spent three months in jail for it. I saw Traci Lords on Saturday, in front of that club Saturday Night Fever on Hollywood Boulevard. Anthony just walked in and dropped twelve beers on the floor by accident.

This weekend's summary:

Friday night: *Birdie was finally ready to go out at one in the morning! She always takes three to four hours. We sat in the car, smoked a joint, went to IHOP for a sandwich, and then turned around and went home! We never even made it out because she took so damn long. I could've killed her! It was a waste of an outfit and makeup.*

Saturday night: *Picked up Birdie. Went to Saturday Night Fever. Got caught in gang territory before we went in* *(smoking another joint and doing vodka shots in the car). We were running in our high heels because we heard gun shots and didn't want to be caught in the middle of something. There was a huge line that snaked around the block, but we were pulled to the very front and let in straight away. Courtney Salzberg was in line with her friends and asked me to get her in. I said I couldn't, and waltzed past the velvet ropes while she stood out there with the masses. Danced up a storm to songs like "More, More, More" and "He's the Greatest Dancer."*

Sunday night: *Club Seventies with Lisel and Missy. Very cute guys bought us drinks all night. Spilled a few on myself dancing to* Grease *songs with Lisel. She took her pants off at the bar. I danced on the main platform with Theodore; there was a huge spotlight on us. He wore his afro wig and bell bottoms. Missy drank too much and ran in front of a huge truck on Highland. The truck screeched to a stop. Then Lisel got really pissed on the way home and jumped out of the car when we were stopped at a light and walked off into the night in her two ponytails. These bitches are crazy. Lovable, but fucking crazy. Anthony is gone for three months on a movie job. I am so relieved. Trying to keep up on watching the O.J. Simpson trial. There is no way he can be found innocent, but it is entertaining watching the lawyers make their case. The guy Missy is seeing, a ZBT fraternity guy named Jordan, saw the white Bronco police chase in person last year; they were on the 405.*

Journal Entry 2/8/1995

Tonight Missy wanted to go spy on Jordan. She is convinced he has a girlfriend. We wore disguises; wigs to be exact. She wasn't quite sure where he lived so we went searching around Wilshire and the 405 for a while. She eventually recognized his place and I got out of the car and pretended to be a jogger and slowly jogged by his house in the dark night. The front window was completely open- I could see everything! I saw his girlfriend and him on the couch watching TV...and then I noticed the stroller. Missy is in shock that he has a kid. Now it all makes sense. She said she called once and she heard a baby crying and she thought she had the wrong number. Another time he had a car seat in his car, but he said it was for a nephew. She is really upset.

Journal Entry 2/13/1995

I spent all weekend with Birdie. She is so beautiful that it is hard to walk around with her sometimes. And yes, she was beautiful before, but now she is even more striking. She has lost weight. Her hair is almost to her elbows and is a light champagne blonde, which looks fricking dazzling against her dark skin. Her eyebrows are perfectly done and her lips are heart shaped and glossed with a bubble gum color. Her eyes are huge, her nose is tiny- she looks like a Barbie doll.

We went to clubs this weekend, stoned, drunk and on Vivarin. Saturday night's buzz was perfect. A Vivarin, a few shots of Rumplemintz and a few hits of pot before we went into the club. Then a lot more drinking. Missy was with us one of the nights. The stories of this weekend aren't too interesting. We got picked out of the crowd, they put V.I.P. wrist bands on us, and then Birdie screwed up all of the info on her fake ID when they questioned her. They let her in anyway. Guys were all over us, either

*clapping when we walked by or saying "YES!" or "yeah!"
or "thank you for wearing that **shirt**!"*

*I started feeling all good about myself- which always
backfires on me. I said, "I'm **sorry** but, we are like, the best
looking girls **here**," while re-applying my vanilla frosting
lip gloss. Birdie's eyes were bugged out and she covered
her mouth, while staring at my lips. It wasn't my lip gloss I
was applying; it was my black liquid eyeliner! I am always
put in my place.*

Although Birdie was from a rougher Hollywood
background, as I was, she did have a family, and had a
certain amount of class if you can believe it. The girl knew
how to project an image. She ate very properly and slowly,
knew her manners, and was able to be feminine and
ladylike when she wanted. Her parents had her in private
schools and took her to Europe often as a child. In spite of
all of that, she was self-destructive. She would pop any
pill; do any drug put in front of her. There was something
missing inside her; she did not care about being safe. The
normal instincts that pop up in the rest of us were not there
for her. She was game to try everything. When I watched
her, it felt like she was playing chicken with the universe a
lot of the time.

That particular year we were both obsessed with being
thin. We would eat a ton of pizza and go back to the
dumpster behind my apartment building and throw up as
much as we could get out. I think she asked me to show
her how to make herself vomit, and being the great friend
that I was, I showed her how to damage yet another part of
herself.

She mostly stuck to not eating at all. That screwed things up one night when we were going into a club. As the guys checked Birdie's ID, she suddenly started wobbling. The next thing I knew, she fell over backwards. She had fainted from not eating the whole day. The bouncers peeled her off the ground and booted us out, saying they couldn't have anyone on drugs in the club. I dragged Birdie back to the car. She didn't care that she fainted; she just wanted to know if she looked fat when she fell. She was grilling me, saying, "Are you SURE I didn't look fat when I was on the ground?! Swear on your LIFE!"

After nights at the clubs we would often wake up in the morning and go to the beach. Birdie wore a full face of makeup and gold stilettos in the sand. I knew she struggled with the same thing I did: We didn't know how to be normal. It is very hard to un-Hollywood-ize yourself.

As for me, I hid behind my looks and hoped no one probed any deeper to reveal my many flaws. I hadn't learned the many lessons I needed to learn: how to treat people, how to behave in society, general courtesy; the list went on and on.

Journal Entry 2/18/1995

I just looked at the tag on the powder blue halter top I wore out last weekend and the name of the clothing line was "Feel the Emptiness" and on the back of the tag it just said "numb" instead of laundering directions. Interesting. Well, Poppy is running from her Sicilian mafia "friend," aka sugar daddy, Vince. He is after her to bust her legs or something because he bought her a car and she wouldn't sleep with him. She had to hide out at my place. I don't know if she promised to be with him and then went back on it, or what, but whatever she did, he is pissed.

Last night, Birdie and I were approached by a USC football player who said he would pay us to do stuff while he pleasured himself. He was dead serious. We told him to fuck off. I thought it was weird- he was attractive and young and rich- why would he do something like that? It was just ugly.

I am sitting here in a Charlie's Angels *T-shirt that is ten sizes too small and boxer shorts. I have figured out that smiling a lot is getting me everywhere. The snobbiness that Birdie prefers sometimes works against us. Missy's way, just being majorly happy, gets you everywhere (and Missy is never even trying to get anything off anyone, unlike Birdie and I, who are always trying to scam drinks.)*

Warren G is on the radio, singing "This DJ." It reminds me of last year. Summer time. Pool. Working on the patio at lunch. Eating sub sandwiches. Drinking Gatorade.

Journal Entry 2/21/1995

Matt Le Blanc from that TV show Friends *was trying to pick up on me last night in the V.I.P. room at Saturday Night Fever. I think he is really cute- but I got nervous. I patted him on the chest and just kept walking. He didn't let it go at that- he came up to me again, flashed that smile, and just stood in front of me, locking eyes with me. Whenever someone is really super cute I can't even talk to them or look at them, I turn into a twelve-year- old again and get all flustered.*

I broke down today. I thought about the last time I felt actual joy, and it was in 1983, when mom and dad bought my sister and me kites. We flew the kites as a family, over the bumpy green hills and under the warm pink summer sky. I miss it so much, it hurts.

Dad used to take us to Zuma beach and let us swing really high on the long swings. Once I got myself pumping on the swing, I would wait until I swung forward and then would launch myself through the air. It made me so happy to be in the air for that moment. It felt like time stopped for a second; then I would hit the hot sand with a thud. My dad would go to the food stand and buy us these huge jawbreakers called Dinosaur Eggs. It was one big egg in a small black cardboard box with colorful writing. I had that thing in my mouth while swinging and jumping with the bright yellow sun in my eyes, flip flops on the sand next to me, the sounds of Culture Club's "Do You Really Want to Hurt Me" coming from the teenagers in the parking lot.

Nothing can top those feelings of actual joy. No buzz is equal. No star hitting on me, no compliments, no free drinks, no nothing can compare to the feelings I felt when my family was together and I felt safe. Now I look at myself...random bruises healing (I fell down some stairs on Sunday night), face puffing up from booze, bong sitting on the coffee table, empty bottle of schnapps on the ironing board. Phone book packed with phonies, dishes piled up, diet pills jumbled up by the alarm clock, a rainbow of bras and g-strings thrown throughout the apartment...

I had all of these relatives on my dad's side. They'd all barbecue and drink beer and listen to The Oak Ridge Boys and Juice Newton and Kenny Rogers, with their big beards and moustaches; their wives in tube tops and feathered hair. Someone was always playing the acoustic guitar and there was always a dog with a gooey tennis ball in its mouth, waiting to play. I would have to take the ball by the tips of my finger nails so I didn't have to hold the neon green mush.

It was the early 80's. My sister and I ate bright orange tangerines off the tree in the backyard, which sprayed us with a sweet mist when we tore them open, stinging our eyes. We desperately wanted to dig a tunnel underground, but the dirt would always cave in on us. We would watch Pippi Longstocking *and then run outside and pretend we were trying to escape from bad guys who were after our bag of gold...*

I had a sticker book full of round scratch n' sniff stickers; vinyl pencil cases with secret compartments, and tiny candy-smelling erasers that I used as hopscotch markers. I got up when it was still dark to watch Saturday morning cartoons (only Davey and Goliath *was on that early) and watched* The Dukes of Hazzard *every Friday night while eating pizza...*

I have to stop thinking about it. Things change, people change. Everyone has to grow up.

LIKE A FLEA ON A DOG'S ASS

It was the summer of 1995. Poppy needed a place to live,
because she was running from that sugar daddy of hers
who wanted his car back. Ah, such is the stuff of life for a
Los Angeles girl.

I let her move into my room and pay half my rent. It was
fun, sort of like a slumber party. Anthony still had the
other room and paid the rest of the rent. If you think I
started saving money or somehow being wise with it, you
are crazy- I went straight to the Sherman Oaks Galleria
(which, incidentally, was the very same mall that was
featured in *Fast Times at Ridgemont High*.) It was caddy
corner to us, so I rushed my ass over there and bought
more club clothes. I was convinced pastels were going to
solve all of my problems.

One day, Poppy and I went to the beach and she pointed

out that we were being followed. I hadn't noticed, but then again, I was never running from guys named Vince who gave away cars. The next day her car was gone. We looked everywhere for it and it was flat out missing. She couldn't report it stolen because it probably wasn't under her name; if anything, *she* could probably have been charged with theft for stealing the damn car from Vince. Nevertheless, without a car she was laying around the apartment quite a bit. Every time I came home, she always seemed to be reading the yellow pages, her French tip manicured nails gripping the bending yellow paper while her long strawberry blond hair spilled onto her bony shoulders and huge oversized boobs. I found it odd, but it seemed like it made her feel like she was accomplishing something, so who was I to interrupt. She also talked incessantly about needing to get her jaw operated on. It was all she talked about for a while. I just stared at her. I didn't get it. Her jaw was fine- she didn't have a crazy underbite or overbite, it was totally average, if not above average.

In the weeks to come, she was on a private mission. She called up a plastic surgeon she used to date and tried to get back into his life. Her green eyes were twinkling- she rather enjoyed swindling guys. I think it was fun for her. Anyway, she was thrown a curve ball: he had a new girlfriend, a college girl from Pepperdine, who was nineteen. She wasn't going to let the nineteen-year-old take away her meal ticket. She needed that damn jaw fixed and she was convinced this old bag of bones would be the one performing the surgery- and performing it for free. When it wasn't looking good, she tried another route: she announced she had TMJ. She hoped to make it a medical concern so she could get it paid for by the state, but no one was buying it. It was all very odd. Needless to say, I tried to stay out of her hair.

Journal Entry 2/28/1995

All is well with Poppy. As long as she stops using my conditioner, I will have no problems with her. She is nice and all, but I am sick of her talking about all of the things she is going to take care of and then watching her sit on the couch the entire day and read those damn yellow pages.

Birdie and I went to El Compadre last night. Saw Quentin Tarantino and Uma Thurman having dinner. They are both really big right now because of this movie Pulp Fiction *that came out last year- Blake used to quote that movie every five minutes- he was so annoying. Anyway, I went to a Jacuzzi party last night and caught a chill. It was a bunch of drunken strippers pouring champagne in their mouths. That USC football player who approached Birdie and me last weekend, approached us again this weekend. He took out a huge wad of hundreds and shoved it in my face and asked me how much it would be just for me. Me and him. He just stood there, glazed looking and slurring with a dark drink in his other hand. I said, "Look, I am not a prostitute."*

I ate well today: An orange, steamed vegetables, four strawberries, 1 ½ grapefruit, and one bowl steamed brown rice. Don't feel happy for me just yet, because yesterday I ate two soft tacos, a half a bag of Trader Joes pretzels, six shots of vodka, a glass of champagne, three pieces of pizza, a foot long meatball sandwich, a bowl of fried rice and a ton of other shit (I know.)

*I used to die for TV dinners when I was a kid. They came in foil trays and were baked on a cookie sheet. My sister and I loved them because they often came with a little brownie, but the **best** part of them, besides getting to eat them on TV trays, was the mashed potatoes. They were fucking delicious. They probably weren't even real potatoes, but no matter, we ate them up like they were a rare delicacy from the South of France. My sister and I were in very few fights as children, but one of them was over those mashed potatoes. I swiped my finger through hers to steal some and the next thing I knew, we were punching each other. They were **that** good.*

I remember polishing off a can of that squirty cheese (in the bottle) within a matter of an hour or so. Why? Because I would make very elaborate designs on crackers, of course. I would try to make a swirl on the cracker, a perfect swirl that took up every bit of space, and then I would swirl and swirl as it got higher and higher and higher... It was that very design that usually caused the can to run out. I would then panic, because it was usually a Saturday morning while watching cartoons, right after my mom had returned from the store with the food. She would get pissed if you polished off something the same day it was bought, because it was supposed to last the whole week.

Sometimes my mom would buy us sugary breakfast cereals. It was very rare, though. She tried to keep it healthy. I liked the sugary cereals not just because they were sweet, but because I loved the colorful cartoon packaging and the commercials for the cereal. The box for Fruity Pebbles was my all-time favorite. If the box had been all white with some black writing, I would have not wanted the cereal as much.

*I remember wanting the toy that was advertised on the box- and wanting it **ASAP**. I don't think I ever waited until we ate the cereal down enough to actually pour the toy out into the bowl. I always opened the box and dug my dirty hand straight into the cereal and got that bad boy out right away. I also ruined the shape of the box by doing that; it ballooned out in the middle and I couldn't get it back into its original shape. I was also known for ripping the little flap and insertion part so that you couldn't close the box properly. Anyway, it was always a rush when I saw the little plastic toy wrapper poking out of the cereal, despite the fact that the toy was usually a cheap version of what was promised on the box.*

Journal Entry 3/4/1995

I am waiting for Birdie to come and get me. She says she has been hanging out with Bobbie Brown, that girl from the "Cherry Pie" video- she has a little baby. I am wearing the "Feel the Emptiness" halter top. "Numb."My car died today. I don't care. It's gone. I should have known that would happen. It was making all of these noises, but I just kept turning up the radio so I didn't have to hear them and worry. I can be like that with my health too- if I see something wrong with me, I just cover it up, keep going and try not to think about it.

I had an incredible nightmare the other night that scared me so badly that I couldn't shake it off. I woke up quickly and realized I was going straight to hell. I prayed so hard I was practically bawling. It was a long dream and I was depressed for a few days afterward. I am scared right now, with my hair in this ponytail, my face caked with dark pan cake makeup, the taste of vodka in the back of my throat... Can it be so wrong to be young and partying? Isn't this standard? Or is it too much? I should find some way to better myself, do some charity work or something. Help some kids somewhere. Go to church or something.

Journal Entry 3/6/1995

That Saturday night I mentioned above turned out to be crazy. Birdie and her platinum blonde, big-boobed friend Shannon came and picked me up in a new white BMW. We then proceeded to pick up these two guys up in the Hollywood Hills and we all went to Saturday Night Fever. I ended up wearing a tight yuppie sweater and a tennis skirt. People were plopping down money to buy us girls drinks and Birdie and I got wrist bands to go into the V.I.P. room. Shannon didn't. They are really strict. Christina Applegate was in there. She is so much smaller in person.

At the end of the night, Pamela Anderson of all people came into the ladies room in a white dress, and did her makeup right next to me. I was leaving the same time as she did and I saw that Tommy Lee was waiting for her outside the door, and I guess guys were yelling stuff to her as she walked out. Tommy did not appreciate that, and some pushing ensued. Next thing I knew, there was a mess of bodies flying- a huge brawl broke out.

It was dark, so I didn't see where Tommy disappeared to, but I noticed that the two dorks that we came with were suddenly in the middle of the fight. Five security guards stepped in and some ass-kicking commenced. I smashed

*myself into a corner with Pamela Anderson while Birdie
drunkenly stumbled to get involved. It was such a mess.
The brawl went on for a good ten minutes and a huge
crowd formed. Birdie's "date," this idiot who is like, two
feet tall, got beaten down with one of those huge black
heavy flashlights and then thrown outside. An ambulance
came because his damn head was split open. We were
standing over him in the rain and blood was pouring out of
his skull. Some chick was holding his forehead together. I
had to make a statement as a witness. Birdie accidentally
got popped in the mouth and was spitting blood. The other
guy we were with, some fat ass, was hiding in the bushes,
and wanted me to get his shoe. I slid in blood and rain to
get it.*

*Right now it is really quiet. Poppy is resting and we are
waiting to watch* The Jerry Springer Show *at 11:00. She
loves that damn show. I was watching entertainment shows
like* Extra *and* Entertainment Tonight *and had to stop
myself from name dropping all of the people they show
who I have run into at clubs or waited on at work. I used
to be into TV a lot more than I am now. I must've logged
thousands of hours watching* Little House on the Prairie. *I
am pretty sure I have seen Mary go blind 80 thousand
times. I really liked episodes with Nellie Oleson (rich,
blonde villainess.) Her red bows were the only damn color
in the show. I liked Miss Beatle, the teacher. I could smell
her Lemon Verbena perfume right through the TV. I also
thought Albert was kind of cute when he was young, but
not when he was older and hooked on Morphine and
throwing up. I think the show I loved the most though, was*
Growing Pains. *Who could forget the episode where Mike
wrote all the answers to his test on his shoes and then
foolishly kicked up his feet on his desk when he got an A?*

*And who could forget Mike's best friend Richard Stabone,
aka **Boner**? Maggie and Jason Seaver were cool parents
and seemed so in love. Carol was a little histrionic but I
liked her red glasses.* Who's The Boss? *was another great
show. Tony Micelli always behaved as if he had done an
eight ball of coke, Mona was a big ol' ho and Samantha
had cool clothes. Everyone waited for Tony and Angela to
hook up!* Mr. Belvedere *was right up there with* Growing
Pains. *They weren't as loving as the* Growing Pains *family
though. Mr. Belvedere would write in his diary each night
at his desk. I hated that he couldn't do a better job
pretending to be writing. He just skimmed the pen in
straight lines across the pages.*

All the girls I knew loved to watch Punky Brewster. *I
remember hearing about the audition for that show
through the grapevine in our neighborhood: a bunch of
blondes showed up and everyone was surprised that a little
dark haired girl got the part. Don't people know blondes,
especially blondes with money, are the **villains** in 80s'
sitcoms and movies? The only exception was* Silver
Spoons. *Even Blair from* Facts of Life *was the one to hate,
at first. Molly Ringwald could have **never** been blonde!
How could you have rooted for her? Anyway, we all loved
when Punky lowered her golden retriever down from her
tree house in a basket. What was that dog's name?
Brandon? I was always disturbed by Punky's back-story,
even as a kid. Her mother left her at a fuckin **shopping
mall**? And they let an **old man** adopt her ass? It somehow
still turned out all sunshine and rainbows.* Small Wonder
*was a really low budget show that looked like someone
filmed it with their camcorder. It was about a robot
masquerading as a little girl named Vicky and her family
had to keep it a secret from their nosey neighbors. I*

remember being annoyed that they didn't let Vicky change her outfit. I got sick of that red dress and white pinafore. It was the same way I felt about Holly on Land of the Lost: *If they didn't change her outfit soon, I was going to stop watching.*

I got bad tips today, even though I was on the patio. Everyone told me it was because it was Monday. There is always some excuse as to why you make no money when you are waiting tables. It's Monday. It's the Friday before a holiday. It's friggin' Passover. There's a basketball game on. People aren't eating out this week because of the stock market.

I am bored with my life; truly bored. Day to day I sit here and worry about my weight. I am not living, I am just alive. I am full from Saltine crackers and grapefruit. My nails are pastel pink and look like patent leather. My skin broke out from the Valium I took on Friday with P.J. at work (a.k.a. Johnny Knoxville). A roach just came out of my closet. It was a baby. Great. Maybe it can become pals with the rats inside the ceiling.

Journal Entry 3/27/1995

I went to this wedding on Saturday. I agreed to be some Hollywood guy's date, whom I hardly know. His name is Ricky and he used to hang on The Strip back in the day, and he always says, "What's up Jiggums?" I don't know what the hell that even means. Anyway, he is harmless. I think I just went to amuse myself and for a change of pace. I ended up spending eight hours with his ass. His sister was getting married and he was in the wedding. I met his entire family, old friends, baby sitters; the whole thing. So

*anyway, this total disaster strikes at the wedding,
beforehand: Ricky's mother started crying because her ex-
husband brought the women he had been cheating on her
with! The nerve of that prick. His mother broke down. No
one knew what to do, so of course, I pushed my way in the
room and handled the situation. I was like, step back
people. I told her, "You need to hold your head up high
and laugh and have a great time! You are beautiful! Do
not let him see you cry! That old hag- please- you are
much better than her." The family stayed away and let me
do my thing. Ricky couldn't believe I was in there handling
his mother with finesse. I may not know many things, but I
know how to deal with crazy shit like that.*

*I got home from that wedding at ten, threw on a school girl
outfit (knee socks/mary janes, pleated black mini skirt and
a fuzzy, baby pink sweater) and jumped into Birdie's new
car and went to Saturday Night Fever. We stayed until
4:00 a.m. and I had to wake up at 8:00 to go to a work
meeting. We fell asleep in her car in the Del Taco parking
lot. People were looking at us through the car windows in
the morning and thought we were dead. There were fries
all over the dashboard.*

*I got through with the work meeting at 10:00 and we hit
the beach by 11:00. We split a Valium, smoked some pot,
and then passed out all oiled up. I saw that the sun was
going down at some point and I knew I had to work that
evening. Birdie was drinking vodka on top of all of that
and couldn't wake up to get me back home at a decent
hour, so needless to say, I didn't have time to shower. I
had to run into work barefoot, sandy and with messy hair
(and not to mention stoned.) My boss was very pissed
because the work meeting was all about how the*

employees need to come to work presentable; not get ready when they get there. I was so busted, sitting there all sunburned.

Right when I got off work I went to Club Seventies with Missy and her German friend Gretchen, who was thrown out an hour later for falling on her face on the dance floor, drunk. She was like rubber, laughing and collapsing everywhere. She looked like a wild Barbie doll. She is very beautiful and carefree. Her blonde hair is always kind of messed up and tousled and she is always tan and wearing something fuzzy and leopard with thigh high boots. She has a tiny diamond set into one of her eye teeth, so when she smiles, there is a literal sparkle (there should be a ding! sound effect). She looks very Hollywood, even though she is from "JARMANNNEEE." She says all "ayemarican ga-urls have fake breasts."

Journal Entry 4/1/1995

*I spoke too soon about Poppy. She is doing **something** for $500 a day. She is supposedly an assistant to a famous porn star who I just saw on a talk show today. We think she is doing more than 'assisting' because she brought her radio and her dance bag with her. The fact that she isn't a stripper and **has** a dance bag is already incriminating enough. I am about to kill Anthony's cat Patrick- he is tearing around all crazy and ripping most of my pictures of Stephen Dorff off the wall. He is acting out because Anthony threw him in the shower and turned on the water to "discipline" him.*

Journal Entry 4/14/1995

*I went to the gym at 8:30 this morning and then to the mall
with Poppy at 10:00. I didn't have to work today so I came
home and slept. Birdie and I met platinum blonde, busty,
gold-digging Anna Nicole Smith at The Gate on
Wednesday. She had a Texas drawl and was slurringly
drunk in a long, lavender dress with a cast on her arm. She
looked so tall! Birdie said, "Everyone always gives you
such a hard time but I think you are so beautiful." She
thanked Birdie and was all sweet- I thought they were
going to become best friends. Pauly Shore came up to us in
the V.I.P. room, where we were getting free drinks. We
ignored him. The guy who runs that burlesque club Grand
Ville, Josh Richman, asked me to dance for them. He said I
didn't even have to audition. I was flattered, but I would
be too nervous to do something like that. I made a joke and
said I would do it if I could come down from the ceiling in
a gilded bird cage with a powder blue feathered costume.
Met a hot guy named Max, who seems to like me.*

Regarding Max: At first, I thought, *eh, whatever.* But then
I heard that he was a big name around town. He was
popular and rich and only dated the most beautiful girls.
He drove a black convertible Mercedes and everyone knew
who he was, except for me and my Hollywood girlfriends.
I started talking to one of the rich Valley girls at work
named Charlie and she was impressed that Max liked me.
She went to school with him and seemed to know a lot
about his crowd. I suddenly became interested in him and
started taking his calls.

I started going to the clubs with Charlie. She had high
cheekbones, thick eyelashes and long, dark hair. She kind
of looked like a less made-up Kim Kardashian, if I had to
think of someone to compare her to.

I didn't notice at first, but the more I went to the clubs with her, the more I saw how cruel and ruthless the people actually were. They seemed to care *much* more about money than I was used to. Your car was *everything* in L.A. No one ever saw where anyone else lived, and purses and shoes weren't a big deal at that time. There was no real way to tell if someone had money, except to look at their car. It was the marker of one's status. I felt terribly embarrassed of myself for being poor. I was terrified Max and his crowd would find out I didn't have a car and ostracize me. I felt so happy to be in Charlie's black BMW every weekend that I nearly pee'd my pants with relief every time the valet brought it to us. I felt pretty and popular just being in her *vicinity*.

There was something about the world of Charlie and the other rich Valley kids that felt very 'small town.' Their reputations were *very* important. They were permanent fixtures in L.A. and had ten years of reputation behind them that deemed them cool or uncool and there was no wavering from that. They knew the background of everyone else at the clubs, who dated whom, who went to what school and all of that. In my old Sunset Strip scene, the people were always very up and down; you could be 'in' one day and 'out' the next. Not only that, but the cast was always changing; new people were always arriving and people would often disappear. It was very different. I was a mystery to the L.A. rich kids because I appeared out of thin air as far as they were concerned. They knew nothing of my background, but they saw me linked up with Charlie, who had a good reputation. She was a pretty, rich, good girl; no one had an ounce of dirt on her and all the guys drooled over her. I was going to make sure I stuck onto her like a flea on a dog's ass. I needed that credibility.

I had to grab that rung, that trapeze. It was what I had been searching for since the minute I left Hollywood: someone to teach me how to be presentable and how to behave. I was obsessed with learning these things; things that no one talked about; things that seemed to be a secret code of certain families. Families that my family never knew; families we never associated with.

Charlie offered me little tips and hints and I eagerly listened to her. She told me not to show my abs so much and not to have too much cleavage. She thought I wore too much makeup and that I looked better with less. I nodded and soaked it all in. I was sure that everything I was doing was wrong and everything she was doing was right. Period. I didn't want to keep even an ounce of myself, I wanted no trace of what I was. I wanted to change into someone like her.

I knew I was more attractive and thinner than I had been in the past few years, but that was only the tip of the iceberg. I had a lot more to observe, learn and implement. I finally had a teacher, and I was convinced her words were from the heavens.

I started to let Charlie dictate *everything*. Once she was aware that I was completely open to being taught and remade into a different person, she didn't hold back. Some of her advice was brutal: I needed a nose job. I needed to use the stair-master. I needed a different hair style. I needed to exfoliate my skin. And I was always a carrot stick away from being fat. It made me increasingly obsessed with my appearance and what I looked like to other people. It was a cause of sadness along with my other issues. My high from feeling "pretty" a few months prior was quickly fading.

Nine

AN ANNOYING CHAPTER OF NAME DROPPING

It was the spring of 1995 and I was hanging with long-haired, brunette Charlie and her rich friends. At one point, Scott Caan of *Ocean's Eleven* was going to clubs with us; I think she knew him from school or something. He was cocky and bold and liked the pretty girls, no doubt. She was also friends with that guy Seth, aka Shifty Shellshock, from the band Crazy Town. He wasn't full of tats then, he was a cute little baby-faced kid who wore a Frank Sinatra type hat and would always book it to the dance floor when he heard The D.O.C.'s "It's Funky Enough." There was a point in time when we were hanging with Danny Boy from House of Pain and a few of the guys from Cypress Hill, because Charlie was dating one of their friends. I don't remember where they lived or which of their houses I was at, because I was pickled in vodka, but I think a few of them shared a place-I can't remember. I just remember it was a nice house in earth tones and they were polite and pretty normal. I still have a pair of House of Pain sweats that one of them gave me, that I wear when I am on the rag.

I remember running into Stephen Baldwin at Grand Ville. He was always in a jovial mood, and once shoved a bunch of dollars in my cleavage. I took them and bought myself a drink.

I also recall seeing Leonardo DiCaprio at all of the afterhours/ underground clubs. We saw him around quite a bit. He wasn't all that big just yet, but he was big enough to bring a bodyguard with him. He kept talking to Charlie one night; I couldn't tell what he was saying over the loud thumping music, I just saw him talking in her ear, as she moved her long, shiny dark hair to the side. She came over to me afterward and told me he was trying to set her up with his big red-headed bodyguard. She was like Uh, NO.

And while I am on the subject of name dropping, I might as well tell you about the night at The Room (formerly Bar One) when an A-list movie actor and former underwear model and his friend, a B-list television star with dimples, tried getting Charlie and me to go home with them. A-Lister wanted Charlie and B-Lister wanted *my* sorry ass. They had a bungalow at the Beverly Hills Hotel, and we were supposed to meet them there. We were totally intrigued and wanted to go, but we knew they expected to sleep with us, so we were scared. We drove up to the bungalow before they got there and looked in the window and saw champagne in a bucket of ice. We peeled out of there as if our pants were on fire.

Journal Entry 4/20/1995

I am depressed today. I have been all week. Max won't call me because I wouldn't sleep with him the other night. I was getting along with him just fine and then he started bringing it up over and over again: 'When are we gonna hook up? When are we gonna hook up?' It was so awkward and uncomfortable. Is this what these 'normal' people are like? Anyway, I am too afraid to screw this up by sleeping around and getting a reputation; I have to be very careful. These people talk. A LOT.

Hung out with Jason Bateman last night in the V.I.P. room at The Gate. I used to love him when I was in fourth grade and he was Derek on Silver Spoons- *I was so not into Ricky Schroder- I was all about Jason Bateman. Anyway, At first, he was a big prude. He wouldn't drink with us and he wouldn't go out on to the dance floor- he said he didn't dance. He told us some sad tale of being laughed at during his prom over his dancing skills or something like that. I swear, not a half-hour after he made that statement, he was doing shots with us and dancing to "Double Dutch Bus." He let Birdie put lip gloss on him; he sat there, intrigued, while she applied it with the little wand. He ended up hanging out with Pauly Shore and together they tried to pick up on any girl that walked by.*

The car dealership just called for Poppy. She drove home a brand new red Mazda RX7 the other day, even though she has no job. I am not kidding you; she got a ride to a car place and came back with a car. There was even a fruit basket in the back. Don't ask me how she did that.

Journal Entry 4/21/1995

Now I am wondering if that car Poppy brought home was

*for a test drive. She has been gone with it for three days
and the dealership keeps calling for her. Maybe she is
trying to come up with the money. A very famous
basketball player from the Lakers picked her up on Sunday
to go out. Everyone in our building was freaking out.*

*I am supposed to hang out with Max at his house tonight. I
have to try to get out of doing anything with him. I wonder
how it will go, being there alone with him at his house. He
had a roommate there last time. I have to try and not be a
tease. I don't know how to do all of this.*

Journal Entry 4/23/1995

*Okay...the Max thing is over. In short, we went to the
movies. He paid for himself (on discount no less by
showing his student ID) and not for me. Luckily, I had ten
dollars on me! Normally I have no money at all when I go
out. We held hands throughout the movie (some submarine
movie I had no interest in) and it was weird for me. I have
never been on a real date like that, you know? In
Hollywood, it would be a group of people, sitting up at
Errol Flynn's old estate, drinking room temperate Jim
Beam and passing around a room temperature liter of
cola. And when I say Errol Flynn's estate, I am referring
to the one that burned down, not some mansion in the hills.
We literally sat outside in the pitch dark at three in the
morning, on an abandoned patio next to a swimming pool,
surrounded by hills, dirt, and trees. I was hanging with a
big clump of musicians and dancers and we would all go
from party to party. You wouldn't know that by looking at
me now, in my angora sweaters and baby colors. I don't
know how kids do this, going on a date. It is scary! What
do you say to each other? How do you talk to a guy sober?*

It really terrifies me.

Anyhow, we went back to his house and he was all nervous and insecure and scared to put the moves on me because he didn't want to get shot down again, I guess. He kept making jokes about how we haven't done it and it made me feel bad. Guys in Hollywood never talked about it like that- they would never say things like 'Are we gonna do it or not?' or hound me like that. Some have hounded me to kiss them, but I was never hounded for sex in such a way, even with the biggest man-whores on the planet. I wonder if all regular guys are like this. It is very uncomfortable.

*Anyway, after all of that bitching, Max said it was okay with him that I wasn't 'giving it up,' but that he was going to move on because he was young and wanted to have fun. I swear, I would have done it already, had he not made such a big deal about it. He tried to be cocky after all of that and said, "I **know** you want me to call you again" and I was like, "No, I **don't**," but of course I secretly did.*

I am now on the phone with Missy. Here is what she says: "Lisel and I just bought steaks and artichokes, I need to light the broiler. We are going to the beach tomorrow ...Oh, I love this yogurt, it's the best...You should come over and have Lisel read your cards. You should...she does them really good...Oh-it sounds like something just exploded in the oven...okay, I'll call you when were done eating and she'll read your cards."

Journal Entry 4/29/1995

I never went to Lisel's to have my cards read, I am too scared of that sort of thing. But Birdie went over and kept asking Lisel to ask the cards if she were going to die young, which Lisel says she wasn't supposed to answer, according to her tarot books, because it is unethical or something- you aren't supposed to predict the 4 D's. But Birdie kept bugging her and guess what card she pulled three times? I don't even want to say it because it scares me.

Went to the beach with Birdie yesterday. Weather wasn't so great. Walked by some skinny teenage boys and decided they had better get us stoned. Birdie says that she can tell by looking at people who has pot and who doesn't. These boys ended up having pot, so we got inside their van next to some surfboards, got stoned, and left. We just got back here and tried to order a large pizza to scarf and barf, but they didn't take checks. It's probably better because I went to Sizzler with Missy last night and wolfed down my whole plate in five minutes and threw it up. She said, "What's the **point***?" When I went in the bathroom to throw up, some other girl had just finished barfing herself. I saw the remnants floating in the water when I went to do the same thing. Only in L.A. do we wait in line to throw up instead of pee.*

Today I am starving but I have a gut, so I am carefully taking my water pills four hours apart. I took two at once one time and I looked in the mirror and screamed. The water around my eyeballs was gone and they were sunken in. I looked like an old man with pop eyes.

Last night I was told I was rude, twice. I have been praying that I could be nicer. I don't want to be this kind of person.

Journal Entry 4/30/1995

Birdie is in San Diego doing some photo shoot; Poppy is in Vegas, probably making some rent; Missy is tanning in Malibu and Charlie is at her big house in the hills, probably smoking a cigarette on the front porch with her cordless phone in her hand.

Birdie just called and is telling me about the photo shoot. Here is what she says:

*"I had soooo much fun today! It was like, a big studio overlooking the city...like, all white...It was like, so much fun! I am gonna wear those hoochie shoes and stretch pants tonight...I was gonna stop by your house last night, but most people don't like it so I didn't. Oh my **God**...we should go to the **beach** tomorrow...we need to get **tan**..." I mentioned that someone had to be the sober one if we went out, because it was scary when both of us were too wasted and she said, "No one has to be **sober**- what's **that** all about? What's up with **thaaat**?*

Journal Entry 5/13/1995

*Today at work, I heard my manager, Howard, say, "Who is this guy? Marilyn, is this your guy?" and I heard her say no. Then I looked up and saw **Max** seated at a table staring at me with a huge smile. I said, "No, that's mine." Howard said, "Look at that shit eating grin." I looked at him over the counter and squinted, shook my head and walked away. I ignored him the whole time and thankfully, there was no room in my section, so he and his friends had to sit somewhere else. I finally went over there with my hand on my hip and a snotty look and said, "What are you* *doing here?" and he said, "What? I can't **eat**? I can eat wherever I want." I said, "Fine. Have a good time," and stormed off. He was there for an additional hour and I didn't even look at him once. All this guy wants to do is be able to point me out to his friends and say he slept with me. Which he DIDN'T.*

Birdie says B-Real from Cypress Hill is asking about me, even though he is dating Carmen Electra. Birdie and I were hanging with them the other night in a V.I.P. room. I can never stop staring at Carmen; she is so tiny and pretty and wears pink and fake lashes... there is nothing worse than someone else looking better in your look than you do.

*Poppy painted the living room peach and bought a big screen TV. I let her have free reign of that room because she doesn't really have a space of her own and I felt bad. But peach? And pictures of **wolves**? As long as she doesn't put up a any dream catchers, I'll be okay. Eh, what do I care.*

I am in bed watching Sweet Valley High *with a headache. We went to her plastic surgeon's place for dinner last night and guess what happened...he drugged us! I had one glass of wine and I could barely walk! You should have seen us trying to drive through the winding streets of Beverly Hills in the dark- it was so dangerous.*

Journal Entry 5/14/1995

*Guys were hitting on me a lot last night- one said, 'Are your eyes real? Are your lips real? Are **you** real?' and someone else called me the finest in L.A., but don't worry, two guys called me fat. This is L.A.; you are **always** too fat* *here.*

*I am in a weird transition period right now. I always
wanted to feel powerful, intimidating, and sexy. When I
was very young, I made myself do things I didn't want to
do, because I thought it was the norm. Then I got a
boyfriend and luckily avoided a slew of men in Hollywood.
But in the back of my mind, even during that time, I
thought women had to be swinging from the chandeliers
naked, doing ten back flips, and landing on a dildo in a tub
of baby oil to be sexy. But it isn't so.*

Journal Entry 6/12/1995

*Poppy's phone conversations are hilarious. Right this
minute she is walking around with her cordless, telling
some car dealer, 'I don't care about convertibles. I just
want a Corvette. I am not interested in a Miata or anything
else. A convertible is not the issue. I will actually take any
color Corvette....except gold.'*

*Yesterday she was babbling about her escort service that
she ran last year. She said she would take the dinner or
Jacuzzi jobs and send the wilder girls out for stripping.
'Well,' she said, 'It was **supposed** to be stripping, but the
guys know what's up. Whatever the girl chooses to do after
she walks in the door is up to her, you know?'*

*I have a fuckin headache from the three coffees I slammed
in order to wake up for work. It has been one year since
the O.J. Simpson murders. That shit has taken over- the
trials are on every day and the news talks of little else.*

I talked to Abby on Saturday, my old buddy from high

*school. She didn't stay on the phone very long because she thought I was totally sketchy. She said, 'You're talking so fast- you're all **over** the place.' I think it is because she now lives in North Carolina, so I sound very speedy in comparison to slow Southern drawls. She always makes me feel like I am nuts. Poppy is in the room now, talking to me about how she is going to have her Corvette and her jaw fixed within the week. So sick of hearing about that jaw. I should break the damn thing with a left hook, and then she can have a real reason to fix it.*

Journal Entry 6/15/1995

Birdie and Poppy have been going on drunken rampages. I encourage them to go off together so I won't be pressured to join either of them.

Anthony was rushed to the emergency room last night because he was throwing up blood, nonstop. It was everywhere. Vomiting up pints of blood is not normal. I am kind of worried; I have goose bumps. The weather is ugly. I am listening to love songs, which is the only thing they play at night.

I just ate some pasta and read as much of the new Vogue *as I could bear without being simply bored out of my mind. I need to digest this food so I can put on my black Everlast sports bra and go running up in the hills of Sherman Oaks. I am looking at my makeup box. There are white sparkly lip gloss tubes and bottles of light pink and white nail polish and little round jars of concealers and blush. There is a basket nearby holding a pile of magazines:* Vogue *and* Cosmo. *I have a big round mirror that sits on the ground and a little makeup mirror in front of it. There are two bottles of Clinique astringent in thick glass bottles with light green caps; flat, wide bottles of pale green Victoria's Secret lotion and little deep blue bottles of hair laminator. My bag from last night is thrown next to my bed (I spent the night at Charlie's after going to the Tea Room and seeing no one interesting.) My room has ceramic angels, antique lamps, many black and white vintage photos, old books and little trinket boxes. There are shirts of pale lavender, baby blue, and light pink on the floor. My bed has white sheets and a fluffy white pillow. My walls are lavender, so is my comforter.*

Charlie came over here to get me last night while Poppy and Birdie were getting ready. They were trying on different outfits and different shoes, fiddling with their hair, and complaining about their makeup. Charlie was in her work clothes from Pao Pao and I had on an Adidas t-shirt and men's boxers. We were just staring at the fuss, even though we had done the same thing countless times before.

Birdie put on some black clogs and asked, "Are these okay?" with a sincere look on her face. She had perfectly smudged black eye liner and one eyebrow up.

Charlie: "They aren't bad, but there are better."

Me: "You need some combat boots with that outfit."

Poppy: "Alcohol is making me swell up-"

Birdie: "Are your downstairs neighbors home? I need to use their mirrors..."

Charlie and I walked outside to her car. "There is so much **glamour** going on," she said, laughing.

Journal Entry 6/16/1995

Poppy and Birdie just got home from last night, wearing the same clothes. Birdie's makeup was all over her face, smeared over one eye. She told me my skin looked really good. I downplayed the compliment by complaining I had bags under my eyes. Right now, they are on the couches in the living room, crashed out. They said they didn't have that much fun last night. They said it was "okay." I am going to interview Poppy. Here it goes:

Me: "Poppy, what did you guys do last night?"

P: "Where to begin...I don't even know the name of the club we went to. What's the name of the place?"

Me: "No cute guys?"

P: "No cute guys, all prostitutes; but there was one good thing..."

Me: "What?"

P: "The drinks."

Me: "How much did you guys drink?"

P: "Half a bottle of wine, two whole glasses of Jaegermeister and smoked some weed and then we drank a beer on the way home in the car. After we got to our next destination, I had a screwdriver and Birdie had a shot."

Me: "Where did you guys sleep?

P: "If I have to answer that you'll faint. You'll kill me."

Me: "But it's for the interview."

P: "I slept next to Michael from Alleycat Scratch all night long. He was a gentleman."

Journal Entry 6/18/1995

It is sunny and birds are chirping. The sky is blue. It is summer in the Valley, once again. Most of my memories of summer are pretty good, but I will never forget that one year- I think it was 1985- Things were tense and scary around the Valley because there was a serial killer on the loose. They called him the night stalker. He wore AC/DC shirts and murdered people and drew stuff on the walls with their blood. I had never heard of anything so horrible and slept with a hammer in my bed. He was breaking in through unlocked windows, so we had to keep ours shut even though it was super hot at night. He had killed some people in Northridge, which bordered our city, so we were scared shitless. I think it was the first time I had a real worry, a real fear. Usually parents tell you everything is going to be okay and not to worry, but my mother was going around and locking all of the windows- I knew it was serious.

Charlie turned twenty-one on Thursday. We went out for sushi with all of her Valley friends who make me uncomfortable. We drank tons of champagne and she opened a bunch of presents in a black silk dress, laughing and spilling drinks on herself in front of her parents. A

*bunch of cameras were flashing. The night before that, we
went to The Gate. Some man ordered us a bunch of
chocolate covered strawberries and champagne. The
morning before that, we lounged around her pool with
some of her other friends. We ate sandwiches and floated
on pink rafts in the clear blue water. Her mother brought a
big crystal bowl of cut watermelon out to us and the dog
ended up eating it. Later I took a nap on her white, down-
filled feather bed. I swear, I sunk down a foot when I laid
down- I wish I had a bed like that. Later on that night, we
got really stoned off a three-inch joint before going out.
Yesterday we went to the beach and laid in the sun, waves
crashing in the distance, the smell of coconut on our skin,
boom box blasting TLC and songs from the* Friday
soundtrack.

*Max called me and tried hooking me up with his sneaky
looking friend Andrew. Actually, Andrew is charming and
attractive, but he still looks sneaky. I made the mistake last
weekend of saying to Andrew, "Well? What's up with
you?" Anyway, Max tried getting me to go over to his
house and hang out with them. That doesn't even sound
correct, hanging out with two guys at a house. I told him I
had to go running that very instant. My neighbor says he
was testing me to see if I would hook up with any of his
friends.*

*I finally saw my mom and grandmother. I was nervous
when they came over. I didn't want them to think ill of me,
so I was trying to prove I wasn't some wild person. And
guess what happened? First of all, Gabriel, Anthony's
friend, walked out in a fucking towel. Then, Poppy came in
to grab something and had a porn star with her, whose
boobs are like, an F cup. My mom and grandma were*

*like...uh...what is going **on** around here? I shut my eyes and shook my head, like, can you guys please get the fuck out of here and let me try to look normal in front of my family?*

I used to love going to my grandmother's house. It was always dark inside, even in the daytime. When I walked in, her eyes beamed and she always said the same thing: "Hi Doll!" and then "Give me un bacio ("oomBAHgzo")" which translates to "a kiss" in Italian. I would run and kiss her, smelling her rose-scented hand lotion. She was quiet, sweet, and beautiful and always wore dark fuchsia lipstick and smoked Parliament cigarettes. I love the smell of them, even today- I know- it is crazy.

She used to seem very glamorous to my sister and me. We always stared at her pictures from her modeling days at Eastman Kodak. She was in hula skirts and sailor suits, with painted-on red lips and very arched eyebrows. We would sneak into her room and look through her big white leather jewelry box full of delicious costume jewelry. Long pearl necklaces, drop rhinestone earrings, brooches and other pins in little satin Chinese bags. She had a lipstick holder on her vanity tray that was a ceramic bust of a girl. It held cherry red and deep pink lipsticks in heavy gold applicators. She had large perfume bottles on her vanity as well: White Shoulders, Youth Dew and some others. She also had a shelf of ceramic piggy banks. There was a bubbly, pale pink one with his eyes shut and a little smile, a small baby blue one with eyes that looked off to the side, and a big terrific white one, a perfect sphere with little painted hoofs and a nice thick cork in his nose. I secretly named all of them and wanted to play with them but I was not allowed.

Dark pink roses will always remind me of my grandmother. She loved growing roses in her beautifully kept yard along with begonias and geraniums. There was a strawberry patch under her orange tree and the berries would get warm in the sun. She loved watching the birds, namely hummingbirds. It makes sense to me now, because she was as delicate, beautiful, and quiet as a hummingbird most of the time. I wonder what she thinks of me now.

Ten

A NICE CHAT WITH
A VIOLENT RAPIST

Journal Entry 6/20/1995

*I think a lot about kids right now. It is summer and they
are running around excited that school is out. They don't
realize what is coming up in their lives. Good for them.
Why should anyone grow up and see any of the stuff I see?*

*I used to love dandelions when I was really little. Big
puffball heads, perfect round balls. I didn't like blowing
the fluff off of them because it ruined the perfect ball and
made it into an ugly stem. A regular weed. It was no
longer special. I also have a faint memory of being two or
so and playing with the game* Operation *and being rather
frightened of the buzzer when I hit the sides. I must have
been no good at that game. I was afraid of the charley
horse and that friggin bucket that represented water on the
knee.*

Everything was so beautiful when I was little. I loved everything about life; it seemed to be so sunny and colorful. There were bursting pomegranates, mud pies in the shaded playhouse, Jiffy Pop popcorn and sparklers, playing house with big pretty dolls with yarn hair and flat faces, doing perfect cartwheels on warm green grass, singing Christmas carols and clutching thick peppermint candy canes...

I loved sleeping in tents on hot summer nights and trick-or-treating for candy in our homemade costumes. I loved the pinks and reds and lace hearts of Valentine's Day. I loved the leaves falling and the Santa Ana winds; wearing ribbons in my hair, climbing up into trees with my Garfield lunchbox to look out over my world. I loved to sit in the window of my bedroom and smell the fruit-scented trees outside while the white curtains ballooned in the breeze.

I think a lot about having my own kids one day, somewhere far away where they can't be tainted. I want to make it perfect for them. That is how I saw my childhood. Perfect. Teenage years, hell no, but childhood, yes. I am watching the news. Lana Turner passed away tonight. Heidi Fleiss is going on trial for pandering. There is a bomb threat on LAX. There was a fire in Riverside that killed a baby sitter and some kids. The last witness for the O.J. Simpson trial will be Nicole's mother.

Los Angeles makes me sad. It's like confetti covered quicksand. You don't notice you are sinking, because there is always a party going on around you, so sensationally slick and "fun."

I don't feel happy being a young adult in my prime. I wish

I were a kid. It is making me choked up. Drinking, guys, tans, beaches, makeup, diets ...How stupid it all is. And I can't even get away from it, I can never go back. I think it's good for me to think about the old days and get sad, because then I briefly remember who I once was. But soon enough, I am back to where I was, falling deeper into a world of emptiness. I wish I could remember things that made me happy as a child more often, then I would not be so sad all the time, so lost all of the time. I am even in a new crowd, and I still feel empty and sad.

Okay, so the craziest thing in the world happened. There has been a rapist in our neighborhood. The cops even put up fliers on our doors with his description: red hair, blue eyes, white male, five foot eight, 160 pounds or something. He was somehow getting through the secure gates in all of these apartment buildings and knocking on girls' doors. When the girl opened the door, he would punch her in the face and let himself in. One of the girls in the building next door was raped. She is one of three on this street alone, which is a street of pretty dancers and actresses, most of who live by themselves.

*So the cops are looking for this rapist. It has been kind of in the background of my life, but I didn't think to write about it. I was at work sitting at the tables by the take out area, where the delivery guys sit. They are from an outside company and we go through them pretty fast. One of them looks about twelve, like a little boy. I talk to him sometimes in passing. The other day he asked me where I lived and I told him the street name without thinking. He said he lived on the same street and I was surprised at the coincidence. He asked me which building I lived in and I told him. Then I asked him which one **he** lived in and he described a*

non-descript building. I said, 'well, what's the address?'
And he didn't know his address. It sounded fishy. He asked
me if I lived alone, and something told me to say I lived
with a boyfriend, so that is what I said. It still didn't hit me
that I was talking to the rapist. He looked so young and
harmless. But then I noticed he had a big scratch on his
cheek and I asked him where he got it. Right at that
moment, it clicked in my head and he saw it click in my
head. We locked eyes. He stuttered and said he scratched
himself on a fishing trip. I mentally ran the description
through my head- oh shit- reddish blond hair...blue
eyes...around five seven, skinny and small for a guy...*This
is him.* And it dawned on me that he was getting into these
women's places because the delivery drivers need the
security codes of people's apartments to get in to bring
them the food. That is how he was getting in the secure
gates. He was obviously making note of the pretty girls he
delivered to, and then going back later, using the security
code to get in, and then knocking on their door.

There I was talking to him, figuring it out right in front of
him. My breathing started to get very shallow, I could not
get enough air. I tried to act normal; I didn't want him to
come after me to shut me up or something.

He never showed up for work the next day. Or the next
day. Or the *next* day. He never came back to work.

I didn't go to the cops. What if I were wrong? That would
suck. But I know I am not wrong. I need to make sure my
door is dead bolted at night. It sucks to be scared all the
time. I can never just relax.

Journal Entry 7/5/1995

Went to Carmella's beach house for the Fourth of July.
She is a dancer at the club Missy and Lisel work for. She
lives on the boardwalk in Manhattan Beach, right off the
sand in a huge condo. It is airy, white, and decorated
nicely. She clearly makes bank dancing. All of the dancers
from the club were there with perfectly round fake boobies,
metallic bikinis, and long hair thrown into ponytails. There
were lots of pierced belly buttons and tattoos. I went with
Lisel (stage name Gia) and we all ate veggie burgers on
the sun deck. Keeping their names straight is confusing
when you are drunk on twelve pina coladas. There was a
delicate faced blonde named Heidi, who goes by Vanessa
'on the west coast.' She wore her hair parted down the
middle and pulled two little pieces to the sides with
barrettes like Marcia Brady. She was snotty. Rumor has it
that she used to date a certain big-time singer who is very
into purple and high heeled boots...

There was a brunette named Leila who brought her five-
year-old daughter who had green hair (because 'it's her
favorite color.' I didn't realize I could have asked my mom
for purple and pink hair when I was a kid.) Anyway, there
was an Asian chick with a total hard-body and an
American flag bikini, who had bad skin. She looked young
and wasn't as close with the other girls. There was a
young red headed chick with a baby, whose name escapes
me and a pretty girl named Veronica who had long, black
hair and bangs. She had a gorgeous Grace Kelly jaw
(Poppy would have died) and a white bikini. She was tan
and somewhat stocky, with perfect boobs. Not very
friendly. There was a burgundy haired, green-eyed chick,
who is infamous in Hollywood. She was pre-occupied. She
is the one moaning in one the Guns n' Roses songs, if I am
not mistaken. She used to do private shows for G n' R that

involved much debauchery.

*Other dancers came and went with ugly grunge guys.
Carmella and I walked through the crowds on the
boardwalk. She is petite and tan with fake boobs and
straight, golden brown shoulder-length hair with bangs.
She has a fresh, girlish face and is always upbeat and
smiling.*

*At night, we all lit a bunch of illegal fireworks on the sand.
Everyone took Ecstasy except for me. Lisel and I were
diving though the air and falling on the sand laughing.
Some guy asked me why I wasn't ex-ing. I said I didn't
want to ruin my skin and have torn up hair. He said, "So
you don't want to do drugs because of your **looks**?" I think
I just didn't know what else to say. The truth is that I am
too scared.*

Lisel was one of the queen bees at the strip club. She did
whatever she wanted, and they let her. There was no
smoking permitted, but she lit up anyway, as if it didn't
apply to her…and it didn't. If men weren't tipping while
she danced, she kicked their cocktails into their laps
without a second thought. One time she was fired, and she
completely ignored it and showed up to work the next day
and continued on. Her bosses kind of bowed down to her
and her pretty friends, and let them do whatever they
wanted.

Journal Entry 7/6/1995

*Lisel, Missy and I went to Raging Waters again on
Monday, which is a water slide park. We laughed so much.
We sat in big yellow inner tubes and rode the waves in the*

big wave pool. I was riding a wave toward a kid who wasn't on an inner tube. My feet were in front of me, coming at him full force and I accidentally knocked his ass **out.** *We ate Dippin' Dots and took pictures in the photo booth. Lisel made us wear sun block. She is mothering like that.*

Last time Missy and I were there, a bunch of gang members were riding the rides. Like, serious gang members from 18th street. They had tattoos that said 18 on their chests and backs and had frickin teardrops tattooed under their eyes and what not. They were intimidating everyone and cutting in lines and people were moving aside for them, of course. No one wanted trouble. Then they came and cut into the line **we** *were in and they got all the way to me. I put out my arm and held onto the railing. The first guy hit my hand and the guys behind him piled up like tattooed dominoes. I turned to the guy and was like, 'you aren't cutting in front of me.' Dude- I know, I am crazy. But it just bugged me. He had a scary look on his face for a second and then I think he thought it was funny. I said they could get behind us, but fuck no they weren't passing me. They saw our boobs and long hair, which I am sure helped in the matter, and then got behind us. We started laughing with them, hanging out, and the next thing you know we were all riding on rides together like best friends. I think we were even cutting in lines with them at one point.*

Journal Entry 7/9/1995

Last night sucked. Went out with Anthony and an old co-worker named Wendy (his fag hag before me) to some get-together in downtown L.A. It was Bor. Ring. I couldn't stop yawning. Friday night I went to some party with Charlie. It was a bunch of young, rich Valley brats who were too young for me to be hanging around (the Valley is so weird- there are really rich people and really super poor people in the same town- don't ask me why.) It was some kid's birthday up in a mansion off Mulholland and they were all hanging out in the front yard by an old twisty tree in the dark. I felt totally out of place; I didn't know their slang or their references, and I just felt like they could **smell** how poor I was. They all kept staring at me. I felt like I didn't dress right or talk right and I was too old. Despite all of that, the young guys were all over me, and I didn't respond, so they started picking on me. One of them was like 'your belly button is an **outie.** It should be an innie.' I said, "There has to be **something** wrong with me," which is probably the snottiest thing I have said in a long time, but I am just sick of people insulting me. It is weird, I get these incredible compliments, but along with them are the worst insults I have ever heard. You would be amazed at the mean things people say to me, many of which I don't write down because they hurt my feelings. Mostly that I am fat, ugly, poor, etc.

Don't ask me about Poppy. I will fill the whole book up talking about how annoyed I am with her. So far this month, she hasn't worked a goddamn day and has been partying every single night. She hasn't paid her half of the rent yet and I am not going to let her live here for free. Nothing is free around here. I have diarrhea and a headache. Aren't those symptoms of some deadly disease? Well, if Anthony and Birdie are still standing, then there is no way I will be going down before those two.

Journal Entry 7/16/1995

I am depressed. I haven't really moved all day. I feel delirious. I went to Fever last night and smoked a totally laced joint with Charlie. I felt like I was going insane. I hope there was no PCP in it...but that's what I get for accepting pot from some black guys in a Saab at the gas station. Charlie said she knew them. Dude, I can see why Rodney King was running from the cops if he was on PCP.

I saw Max at the beach earlier yesterday. He is so good looking. (sighs.) He was at Zuma 6 and I was at Zuma 5 (Zuma is the name of the beach; it's in Malibu, and the numbers are the specific lifeguard stands.) *I hate how everyone knows each other's business. You can't date anyone good looking who hasn't already made a name for themselves, and once they are a name they are like, public property. Everyone is watching them and gossiping. And once you have hit that level where you are one of the names (not saying I am), you have to stay within that class, stick to your kind. The hot girls and the hot guys are expected to date. Because I am now linked to Max, I am being watched. It got around. And the thing is, I don't **want** to be known in the Valley like Charlie is. It is so intrusive. Everyone has the low-down on you. It is all one big high school popularity contest (of which I never was a part) to see who is richest and best looking. It gave me some status to date this guy and it moved me away from looking like a music scene groupie, so that is good. It was good for my image I guess, but what a pain in the ass. I want him out of my life so bad, because I feel myself liking him sometimes and I know it would never work. He would sleep with me, dump me, and tell everyone all the details. I wish I wouldn't run into him everywhere I go. I want to date a bunch of guys, not just be thinking about this one. I wonder when I will stop thinking about him.*

Poppy and I are searching for any kind of sedatives to knock us out so we can get this day over with.

Journal Entry 7/18/1995

*I am lying in bed. I just cussed Poppy out and she is out on the stairs looking suicidal because she thinks she looks like a hag. She told me to get ready four hours ago. **Four hours, people.** I have been sitting here waiting for her! For nothing! I have accepted that Birdie takes that long- she has a very elaborate makeup job to do: false eyelashes, beauty spots, primers, glosses, powders and curling, straightening, spritzing and getting sewn into clothes: fine. That's just Birdie- she has been studying supermodels since she was eight. But Poppy? She spent three of those hours just staring at herself. And she is pretty and has a killer body! She sees something different in the mirror than I do.*

So after four hours passed, she told me she feels too ugly to go out! I am pissed, but I feel sorry for her at the same time because I have felt like that before. I really think she is capable of killing herself over self-hatred. I am not kidding. Eh...I shouldn't have cussed her out probably. Now I feel bad.

Journal Entry 7/19/1995

Anthony is in the shower playing "Get into The Groove" on his radio. Poppy just got home and said 'What if I end up with somebody that is bald or gross because I went for them for their personality? And then their looks went?" I said, "Well, then be like us and don't go for people for their personality." She is talking about her skin now; she says she has lines. She said she smells weed. I said I think it is Anthony's cologne. He just yelled "Poppy!? Will you come in the bathroom and pop a zit on my butt?!"

Jack just walked in wearing a '69' shirt. Now he is trippin' because we are making fun of it. Oh my gosh, he is freaking out. Anthony told him he is being over sensitive and that he wants to borrow the shirt on Friday.

Journal Entry 7/22/1995

*I walked to Pavilions to go grocery shopping. That shit is far away, too. Cheese, lunch meats, and bread are all my favorite foods but were all out of the question for various reasons (fat, sodium, and carbs.) I hate vegetables, so I got grapefruit. Pasta? Too many carbs. Frozen dinners? Too many calories. Juices? No, I can only have water. It was a depressing experience in which I purchased one magazine (*Cosmo*), a pack of gum, four grapefruit and a box of saltine crackers. I came home and re-did my manicure and hand washed some under-things. Then it was time to make my social calls to plan the evening's events. If you are wondering if there is any more to my life, there isn't.*

I continued to wait tables at Pao Pao during the day and traipse around town in pastels at night. Everyone was listening to Tupac Shakur and Notorious B.I.G. in the clubs and doing the new dance, the Macarena, at weddings. The big movies that year were *Casino* and *Leaving Las Vegas*.

Journal Entry 8/12/1995

I have a sunburn and feel hot. I just got pen ink on my

*perfect pink manicure. Today I had to be nice to a lot of people who were either rude to me or ignored me. Table 27 were the usual doctors who all the other servers hate, but who I will wait on. They have no idea what goes on behind the scenes. When they walk in, the servers all talk to each other under their breath. They are too much of a hassle, taking time away that could be used on other tables, and they don't tip to make it worth it- so the servers refuse to wait on them. Usually, one of us needs the money or doesn't mind all that much, and that person is me with this particular group. I bring them their food immediately, refill their glasses with tons and tons of mango iced tea and treat them with top priority and they **still** don't tip me properly.*

There is a man in here almost every day that was hired by the corporate offices. I think he was supposed to come and assess the place and tell them who to fire and who to keep and all that. He is watching all of us and taking notes. He almost fired my ass a few weeks ago for handling my hair in the mirror at the front of the restaurant. For the most part, he is really cool though. His name is Darrin. Jack and I have become close with him. He did something to me the other day that really made me think. He brought me in for a talk, and asked me what my goals were, what I was going to do with my life. I started shifting in my seat. I hate when people ask me that. As if it's just that easy to answer! I said I wasn't thinking about it yet. There was a silence, and then he told me that I should be a career waitress.

I got all upset with him. I felt like crying, because I often wonder if that is what will become of me. He kept pushing it and pushing it. After about five minutes of that, I realized that he was trying to get a reaction from me. He *was trying to get me to think of a plan, so I **don't** become a career waitress.*

He finally talked to me about it. He told me I was too good to be a waitress. He told me to go out and do something big. He told me to get out of there; that I could do better. I started crying. He told me that he dealt with waiters and waitresses all of the time, and that I wasn't one of them. That I was different. I wished he hadn't said that. I don't want to fail. I don't know what to do with myself. It's not as if my dream in life was to become a waitress! It just fell into my lap and I had to survive...who do these people think they are trying to tell me I should be doing something else...It isn't that easy.

Eleven

"I JUST NEED TO SELL THIS HEROIN..."

Charlie was still acting as my personal manager/publicist, and I started to notice her becoming very aggressive toward me as far as who I was seen with. She didn't like my Hollywood friends and she didn't like my co-worker Allison; she thought they were all bad for my image in one way or another. I wanted to tell her to back off, but I was sure my social life would suffer if I crossed her. I saw the way she very suddenly cut off friends, telling all of their secrets to the world and laughing at their insecurities and vulnerabilities. She was pretty vicious once she decided she didn't like someone. Even close friends or family members were not immune. I knew if I was to split away from her that I would have to be very careful about it.

The L.A. club scene was completely different from what I was accustomed, but I realized the formula was the same. It was universal. Don't sleep with anyone. Don't let anyone be able to point you out and say they've slept with you. Bing bang boom. That's it.

After word got out that I turned down Max and he was chasing me, other guys started to chase me, seeing if maybe they could be the one to score. My value rose because of the demand; basic economics were in play.

Charlie noticed that I was the one walking in front of *her* while she trailed behind *me*, and let me tell you, she did *not* like playing sidekick. That was not her gig. The shift in our roles caused her to become mean-spirited toward me. I tried to be more low profile so she could take her place in the spotlight again, but she was being pushed further and further into the background because she started to seem bitchy and bitter, less cute and fun.

I turned twenty-two that fall. Missy's bosses were opening a regular legit nightclub and asked her if she knew anyone who would cocktail waitress. She recommended me, Charlie (who didn't even need to work a second job let alone a first job- her dad was a famous producer- I think she was working out of boredom) and a friend of Charlie's named Carrie Ann. We were excited to pick up some extra money for clothes and shoes and we quickly spread the word about the new club, which was located on Ventura Boulevard. It was one of only a few places to go to in the Valley at that time. Everything else was over the hill, in Hollywood or Beverly Hills.

The opening of the club was a success, probably due to Charlie for the most part. She lent her name to it and brought in many people who either knew her or knew *of* her and considered her credible.

We had to wear cheesy, clichéd outfits: a tight, white, low cut shirt, a short black skirt, a bowtie around the neck and really high shoes. I thought it would be easy not having to remember any food orders, but it was much more difficult than I realized. One, I had to weave through crowds in high heels carrying a tray of drinks. That was scary. Two, it was hard to find the people who *ordered* said drinks. They were moving all over the place and I rarely remembered what anyone looked like. I could never hear anyone over the loud music and I could never keep my money straight. I was horrible at counting back change. It was also challenging because I knew some of the people personally and I felt embarrassed working while they were partying. It was hard being on the other side. So many people wanted to party with Charlie and me. We sometimes got caught up with the whole thing, did shots with people, and then really screwed up at counting back change.

Guys would get drunk and try to grope me while my hands were full of drinks. I had to put my tray down one time, take all the drinks off, and then beat some guy with it. I had this great Austrian bouncer who would throw people out when I gave him the nod. He was hot.

There were also instances where I played bimbo, *deliberately* counting back wrong change to try to steal money from drunk people. I didn't have a conscience whatsoever.

But there were other times where people would get so drunk, they would see their bill and refuse to believe they ordered all of those drinks. We had to sit there while the cleaning crew was cleaning up the place after it closed, lights on, and try to get these slurring drunks to cough up the money. I was like *my dogs hurt; can I get the fuck out of here already?*

Okay, so Charlie and I were there working and partying, but kind of staying separated in our own sections because of the tension between us. We promoted the club on our days off and the bosses loved us for it. They gave us tons of money and free booze. My rent was paid and I had money for clothes. I was stoked. But I was nervous in the back of my head because I didn't have a car and I was feeling the clock ticking on Charlie. I knew she was soon going to turn on me, which would leave me with no ride to work.

Missy worked at the club on different nights. Carmella and the other girls danced on platforms. I did some dancing on the platforms myself and felt really stupid and robotic. Scott Baio came in one of the nights, and Missy started singing the theme song to *Charles in Charge* to him, which he didn't find funny in the least, but I laughed so hard I felt like I did a major ab work out.

Charlie's friend Carrie Ann seemed to be doing just fine at the club, but that was because she was a major drug dealer. She did not need a job, but she wanted to get more customers. She was dealing, among other drugs, the new drug called GHB, which she also drank from a flask from time to time. Sometimes she would pull a huge crack rock out of her bra and order me to step on it and break it with my heel. She would say, "Aye, break this rock, homie." I was like, *is this really happening*? I found it to be absolutely appalling and amusing at the same time. Charlie and I laughed at how crazy she was.

Carrie Ann had a scale and all of the necessary paraphernalia to package and sell drugs in her room at her mom's house. It was all perfectly hidden each time it was done being used. She had this very girly, sweet bedroom where she would measure everything. It was painted in pinks and pale blues and full of pictures of angels and fairies and pretty things.

The owners of the club also used some of us cocktail waitresses to promote their other clubs on the weekends. Some nights just Carrie Ann and I had to go. I didn't want to be around a drug dealer and I especially didn't want to be with her when she did a deal, but too bad for me, she almost always did one when I was with her. I was always praying we didn't get pulled over. She liked to listen to rap, like, Too Short or Eazy E, and the bass would be so loud in her truck that the rear view mirror would shake. If another car was bumping *their* bass loud, like at a stoplight, she would roll the window down and yell, *"Let's have a bump-off, homie!"* and then turn hers up even louder. Then she would grab my purse, open my compact, stuff some drugs inside and snap it shut, all while checking her pager. Sometimes she would be talking to me and would pull out the horn on her steering wheel, fingering around for a baggie of drugs inside.

One day she told me to wait in her truck, she would be right back. I looked out and saw her climbing into her ex-boyfriend's house through a window. She came out quickly thereafter without so much as a change of expression. She was holding a leather organizer full of folded papers. She got back in the truck and slammed the door, tossing it to me. "Aye, hold this." She said it was his phone book and she needed to look up the number of his new girlfriend.

A few weeks later, rumor hit the street that Carrie Ann tied up her ex and his girlfriend to chairs and took all of their clothes. I couldn't imagine how she could have manhandled her ex. Then it crossed my mind that she had most likely used a weapon. I didn't answer my phone for a while.

Meanwhile, back at my apartment, drunken drama was going down. Anthony was dating a cute guy who we were all shocked actually liked him. He never got hot guys or any guys for longer than a night. This guy was polite, young, handsome, smelled good, and drove a Porsche.

I was woken up one night by loud crashing and glass shattering. I jumped out of bed and was nervous to go see what was going on; I was sure it was someone breaking in to finally murder me, which I was always sure was about to happen in that apartment. I was shaking. When I realized it was just Anthony, I started yelling at him. I kept asking him what the fuck he was doing and he kept telling me to go back in my room. I felt really scared- was he going crazy? It seemed like his voice was normal, but he couldn't control his actions. I listened as he shattered potted plants down the stairwell, pushed over his cologne collection on his dresser and knocked over every single one of his belongings.

The next day I demanded to know what was going on. I was furious. He didn't want to talk about it. We got in a big old fight. His behavior scared me really badly- I felt like I was in danger. I didn't feel safe. I wanted him out. I had no loyalty and didn't even consider all Anthony had done for me over the years. He took me with him when we all got kicked out of the Topanga house and he put a down payment on the apartment for us. He had supported my partying for a few years, not to mention food and houseware and furniture. I was ungrateful and remembered nothing from the past. I just knew that I was mad right then. I was mad that he was trashing the place and I wanted him gone.

It turned out that Anthony's hot boyfriend made out with one of Anthony's other close friends- either Jack or his cousin or someone else in their circle, I forgot who. But it hurt Anthony so much he just wanted to throw a fit. I didn't give a fuck and had him taken off the lease and I took over the place. Anthony moved to Vegas and I only saw him once or twice more in my life.

I started dating Max's sneaky looking friend Andrew. He was popular and hot- well, to me at least. Allison saw him around town was convinced he looked like the devil. Anyway, he came at me in a gentlemanly manner and asked me out on a date, so I said yes. He picked me up in a Lexus and took me to Morton's for steak. I was such an idiot that I thought a Lexus was the coolest thing ever. I was trying so hard to act rich; all I wanted to do was be seen in these nice cars so I could feel good about myself. I was quite shallow, but it came from me being so insecure about my social class. It was really very pathetic.

Anyway, I felt this guy was a good match for me. I thought, okay, he has the goods and people know his name. The calculated side of me was pleased that he looked good on paper. But there was something more that I tried not to think about. I got *butterflies* when he looked in my eyes. Right in my gut. *Damn*, I thought, *This guy might get me good.*

I was nervous because I hadn't been on very many actual dates, like I mentioned before. I loaded myself up on wine at Morton's and managed to throw out some witty comments, but I was still terrified and hoped it wouldn't be obvious. I just wanted to be able to be with a guy and not be so *scared*.

He tried to sleep with me on the first few dates and of course I said no. He stopped calling after a bit and then I started to see him out with other girls. It upset me. One time I walked up to him and his date, grabbed his drink, drank the whole thing in one gulp, and slammed it back on the table. Then I took his date's drink, gulped *it* down, and slammed it on the table as well. Classy, huh?

I was pissed. It seemed a lose/lose situation. I just didn't understand. Sleeping with guys made them not call you again and not want to date you as a serious girlfriend. Okay, got that down. But when you say no to sex, you end up losing them anyway? Well *fuck* that. I was getting sick of the whole thing.

Journal Entry 12/7/1995

My new roommate Simon (he used to live downstairs with his brother, but now lives in Anthony's old room) was banging on the door with a seven-foot Christmas tree. I didn't feel too much into the Christmas spirit. I heard him banging from my room and I figured he lost his key, but I didn't feel like getting up to answer the door. I had some music on, blaring from the bathroom, so that was my giveaway that I was indeed home. I was really stoned, a tad paranoid and questioning every friendship I ever had. I didn't feel like being nice is what I am saying. I finally opened the door, looked at the tree, rubbed my eyes, and walked away. When I came out of my room later, he was gone. The tree was up on a stand in the corner and the gifts I bought for my friends were placed carefully around it. It smelled really good so I got a little spark of Christmas spirit, but I still felt lonely and sad.

The next few days were the same. I didn't leave the house, except to go out to clubs at night. Actually, I did go to the store once to get sushi and some Gatorade to mix with my vodka later on. I ran into Max and Andrew at the Century Club and they were trying to cut me down, saying I needed a tan and that I was only nice to people when it was convenient for me. I said "You're right" to both comments. They were hanging out with this really pretty, tan blonde girl named Stacy Ferguson, who used to be on that show Kids Incorporated, *and has since started a singing group with two chicks from my high school, one of whom is Max's ex-girlfriend. They are called Wild Orchid* (and a small note: Stacy later went on to become Fergie of the Black Eyed Peas.)

*I got really drunk after that because random guys were buying me drink after drink. I was even being rude and snotty because truthfully, I didn't **want** any more drinks. I was hoping they would just stop. I was even leaving full drinks at the bar! But needless to say, I got more and more wasted. I went home with Andrew and we got into a huge fight at his house. He was being a jerk because I wouldn't sleep with him. I got so fed up, I did the craziest thing. I said, "Okay, let's just **do it** then. Is **that** what this is all*

*about? Let's **go** then." It was absolutely horrible. I was
really mean afterward, making fun of him. He threw me
out of his house in the rain and I had to take a cab back to
my apartment across town at 5 a.m., in a tiny angora
sweater and little pleated skirt. The cab got a flat tire just
before my exit on the freeway. I screamed at the guy to
shut the meter off.*

*Anyway, I am down and lonely and this weather makes it
worse. So now I am sitting in my apartment with a
poinsettia plant next to me. I am so sick of playing this
whole coquettish thing. I am even more annoyed at how
important this sex thing seems to be. What in the hell is the
big deal with it, anyway! The Hollywood crowd never
made this big a deal of someone not wanting to do it. Ever.
I think I was more friends with that crowd. This crowd
makes it very clear that you are not a friend; you are a
conquest to be had. Well, I screwed up my whole plan,
regardless.*

Later

*I listened to some Christmas carols in the shower. I even
slept out by the Christmas tree so I could smell it. I used to
want to do that as a kid. I used to want to leave the twinkly
lights on all night. It would bother me that my mother
would turn them off when we went to bed. I wanted to
know that they were always on, even when I was in my
room, alone. I especially loved it when it was overcast or
actually raining, but that was rare. It was usually sunny on
Christmas day.*

Birdie invited me to go to Vegas with her that New Year's
Eve. I told her I couldn't afford it and she insisted she had

the whole thing covered. I agreed to go, though I had not one penny in my pocket. She came over and gave me some peach lotion from Bath and Body Works as a little present (it smelled like bananas) and we peeled out like we were running from cops. She smoked pot the entire way there, from a purple bong I got from some guy at work.

We arrived in crowded Las Vegas and walked around the streets with all of the crowds of people getting drunk. When it was time to figure out where we were going to sleep, Birdie revealed that not only did she not have a room set up for us, but had no money either. She told me she was counting on someone buying the *heroin* she brought, and the sale did not happen as planned.

Oh, okay. Okay. You were trying to sell some heroin, I see. Well I totally understand then. Except NOT (shakes head with the sound of marbles rolling around). What the fuck? She didn't even tell me she had drugs on her until we were already there! But this was Birdie. She was probably crazier than anyone I had ever known. I had been uncomfortable with the smoking of pot on the way there, but thought it wasn't that bad…but this…this was scary. Neither of us had money for a room. We didn't even know anyone else out there to try and room with. I was livid. I should've known! I knew I would have to stay really alert when I was with Birdie because we would end up dead if someone wasn't watching.

She approached some random young guys to mooch pot off of them. She whispered to me that we could easily room with them, but I refused. She was a pro at scamming the younger guys, who were so fixated on her beauty that they would empty their pockets immediately, to keep her in their presence for just a while longer. The older ones had her number and required something more, more of a give and take, but the younger ones were easy prey for her. Needless to say, I didn't want to sleep in a room with some strangers. I didn't want to be in this sort of trouble again. I started to realize I would have to stop hanging around her. It was too dangerous. I decided I would have to keep my distance from her when we got home.

She didn't seem all that concerned with finding a place to sleep. She drove us to a crappy unknown casino to use the bathroom. When she came out, she got into the driver's seat of her car and promptly passed out. I looked over at her and she had this thick film in her mouth and was in a deep, creamy sleep. Her makeup was crusted but still beautifully applied. She was still wearing her black and white leopard print fur jacket. I sat there staring at her lifeless body. Then she started snoring like a Great Dane who had just consumed an eighteen pack of Budweiser. It dawned on me that she had probably just shot up heroin because she was out and I couldn't wake her. I didn't know what to do. I was going over speeches in my head, thinking of how I would yell at her the next day. She was in such a coma that we slept right there in the car in that parking lot.

In the morning, people were peering in the car windows to see if we were dead (not the first time this had happened while I was with her). I was pissed. She went into the casino like it was no problem at all, whipped out a toothbrush and brushed her teeth in the ladies room. She fixed her hair and was ready to go on with the day. I was so mad at her!

So the beginning of 1996 was not the best. Waking up in a car was not what I had in mind for the New Year. To top it off, I ruined my social standing in exactly one night. I flushed all of my hard work down the toilet by straying off my plan of abstinence and sleeping with Andrew. Demeaning and belittling him afterward was the nail in my glittered coffin.

He did just as I thought he would. Everywhere I went, I saw him walking up to guys, leaning in toward them with his eyes locked on me, and whispering to them while Craig Mack's "Flava in Ya Ear" or Montell Jordan's "This is How We Do It" thumped through the club in the background. Whomever he was talking to would look up at me and lock their eyes on me, nodding and smiling.

I didn't take that shit lying down. I went up to girls and did the same thing back to him. But I would add in showing an inch with my fingers and pointing at him. Girls would look over at him, but then they would quickly ask me how I did my makeup and hair. I pretended they were talking about him because I knew he was watching. I threw my head back, laughed, and had a few more cocktails. Once I got home though, I was miserable. I cried in my bright kiwi green nightie with a big bow in front, blowing my nose on a sock.

I turned my sights back to Missy and Lisel. When things were tough, I knew I could go over there to vent and I would feel better. They took care of me; they were very sisterly. I knew they had my back. They wouldn't just wake up one day and suddenly hate me, like Charlie would.

They still lived only a few buildings down from me, so I started going over there in the evenings to see what was going on in their world. I loved walking into their well-shaded courtyard full of lounging cats and potted plants. I could often hear music playing and smell grilled food wafting from someone's barbecue.

Lisel moved in another one of the dancers from the club named Taylor. She had a young girl's face and really long dark hair- she sort of reminded me of a young Valerie Bertinelli. She wore long floral skirts, bulky sweaters and very little makeup.

Although Taylor looked like a Sunday School teacher, she didn't act like one. She tried to slide her hand up my thigh one night while I was over there! I expected it from a certain type of girl, but not her. I was stunned. I couldn't move. I felt frozen, like I used to as a young girl when a way older guy was hitting on me and I was scared. I'm not sure why I reacted like that- I guess I didn't want to insult her or make a huge scene. I kind of just pretended it wasn't happening. Her hand got closer and closer to my crotch while we were talking about regular stuff- I felt so awkward. I finally got up and said I had to get going and acted like nothing had even happened.

I sat in Lisel's apartment one evening that winter while she did her toes. Missy cracked open a Diet Dr. Pepper, flipping her long blonde hair off her pretty doll face while they updated me on the issues at their job.

I can't say their issues were anything close to the issues most people have at their jobs. It wasn't like "Oh, we have a new boss who sucks," or "There have been layoffs." I shit you not, one their co-workers had been missing and a dead body was found nearby the club. Then the police identified the body as belonging to the girl missing, a Russian dancer. Lisel was having drinks with her the night before she died. They had traded some outfits (Lisel said there was always trading of outfits, because when you were dancing, your outfit felt played out if you wore it too much.) The Russian girl traded a neon pink velvet dress for something of Lisel's; they drank, they laughed …and that was the last night of that girl's life.

One of the guys from Pao Pao was dating a waitress from Missy and Lisel's work. He told me there was a weird DJ who worked there who had a "hit list" of the people he hated. The dead girl was on his list.

This was one of those things I couldn't comprehend because it was so freaky. I just kept saying…*no…no…this must be some kind of mistake. They have to be wrong about this.* I brought up the DJ to Missy and Lisel and they didn't seem to be worried about him. They insisted he was harmless and an idiot. Lisel said, "**I'm** on his list. Fuck *him.*"

I immediately felt dizzy with worry even though she was tough, and appeared to have had the whole thing handled. I watched as she dangled her long, tanned legs over the side of the bed, waiting for the polish to dry. She combed her pale blonde hair with her fingers, pulling it up into a big bun on the top of her head, dismissing the subject as if it were mere drivel.

Lisel later told me that she had done a side modeling job for the DJ to make some extra cash, and his theme was a little strange: tied up, helpless women.

She also did a modeling shoot with a man who was later convicted of strangling and killing model Linda Sobek. She met him at some car shop for a modeling job; he was a lonely weirdo who was a "car and hot girls" photographer. She drove up to an empty lakebed to do a shoot for him and he took pictures of her at her house another time. When he was there, he tried to touch her and she went off on him and made him leave. Later she saw him on the news and nearly shit her pants- he had taken Linda Sobek to some place in the desert to do some car/hot girl shots and had killed her and dumped her body in the Angeles National Forest.

When Lisel did a shoot, she always made sure the photographer was very clearly informed that she had told people where she was and who she was with. She was a bad-ass; there was no way those mouth-breathing serial killers were going to fuck with her. It was pretty clear she wouldn't go down without a fight. They surely sensed her street smarts, and went to hack *other* poor women to pieces, sparing her. She saw all of these modeling shoots as extra money to survive (she was in some of the big name men's magazines), she didn't realize how dangerous it could be.

Aside from all of that, some other weirdness was going on. Missy was suddenly being harassed by an undercover cop with a porn moustache and thick 1970's glasses. Imagine the scariest, creepiest looking guy you can dream up, and that is what he looked like. The guy had come into their work and busted a few of the extra sleazy girls for lewd conduct and prostitution. They thought that was the end of him. But no. He was a weirdo and started getting super involved in the lives of the girls.

Missy and I found him snooping around her courtyard one day. She feared he was just a dirty cop and would somehow hurt her. Her instincts were right because she started getting weird phone calls and feared someone was breaking into her house. I was scared as shit for her. I was terrified she would end up in a ditch somewhere. I thought that maybe *he* was the person who had killed their co-worker. I felt uneasy. There was always some kind of evil shit going down on my street. There were so many girls without their families, so many girls who were secretive about their lives- they were like fluffy bunnies sitting out in the field, while ugly, drooling, evil wolves came in for the kill.

Back at my house, things were just as sad and secretive. Poppy started running her own personal escort service out of the coat closet in my living room, in between sips of cheap wine.

As I watched her on the phone, wheeling and dealing, I told myself she had to go.

Twelve

ARE WE GOING TO DIE ON THIS SHIP?

Once again, I called my high school friend Amelia. We put the debacle with Charlotte and George behind us and I forgave her for going back on her word to move in with me. She was still frumpy and negative, but endearing. She started complaining that she had no life and loathed living with her mother. We went power walking at night and talked about how great it would be if we lived together. I got closer and closer to her and started to feel like I had another sister. She had a pretty standard, 'normal' life, which I felt would make *mine* less hectic. I ended up throwing Poppy out and letting Amelia take over her spot in my room. She agreed to start paying half of my rent, while Simon continued to stay in Anthony's old room and pay the rest of the rent.

When Amelia moved in, I felt comforted and relieved. Maybe it was because she came with a family attached, which I loved. Or shit, maybe it is because I finally had two people renting from me who had normal legal jobs with W-2 forms. I was a lot less likely to have some angry sugar daddy following me or car dealerships calling because it had been four days since they had let my roommate take their car around the block.

Amelia was blunt and honest and I really enjoyed her company. She even came out of her shell a little while living with me. I always had people over drinking and partying and she got to flirt with cute boys and have some drinks and get frisky. The only thing wrong with that was that she was getting *too* frisky. Sloppy frisky.

I had a bunch of people over one evening to have drinks. We all started getting buzzed and laughing and I realized Amelia was missing. I kicked open my bathroom door to see her making out with my friend/co-worker David. Her face was bright red and she couldn't stop laughing. I kicked him out of the bathroom and yelled at him. She got really sick after that and said she was spinning, so I put her over the toilet and told her to throw up. She couldn't. I told her to stick her fingers down her throat and force 'the poison' out, so she could feel better. People started to come in the bathroom behind us to watch the spectacle. She had no concept of what I was talking about. "Move over," I said, sighing and pulling my long hair back behind my shoulders. I leaned over the toilet, stuck my finger expertly down my throat, and neatly puked in the bowl. I put my head up and saw her turning white. Then she started dry heaving. The next thing I knew, she was throwing up on her own. I jumped out of the way. My roommate Simon was in the bathroom watching and I am not even kidding you, he started throwing up too.

Fettuccine Alfredo in the bathtub. There was a total chain reaction of puke going on.

As for David, cute, happy-go-lucky David. I don't mention him again in this story, but I hung with him a lot more times, going to the beach and to parties with him and his friends. Allison and I were great pals with him, sharing a lot of laughs and craziness. He only lived another few years. His life was cut short by a head injury, a bad fall. We lost him way too early.

***

One of the girls at work invited me to go to The Bahamas around then. She said all I needed to do was buy the plane ticket to Florida, and she had a free hotel room. We would sail from Florida to The Bahamas by boat, which she also had covered. With Amelia slated to cover half of my rent, I was able to buy the plane ticket. I was excited to go on a plane, which I had not done yet.

About a week before I left for the trip, I came home from work a little early and noticed that all of Amelia's things were out of the bathroom. Hmm…That was odd. I saw her that morning and she hadn't mentioned she was going anywhere. I went into my room to take off my Pao Pao apron and noticed that all of her clothes and belongings were gone. The only things left were her furniture and some kitchen stuff.

Just then, she walked through the door with an empty box and seemed startled to see me home. She was on her last round of putting stuff into her car. She appeared to be trying to get it all done before I came home from work. Nice. I asked her what was going on and she told me she wasn't going to live with me anymore. I felt anger rising up inside my chest. Her half of the rent was due the next day. I couldn't cover it because I had bought the stupid plane ticket.

She stood there with the box and told me I partied too much and my hours were too crazy. She said I was too messy and she was sick of cleaning up after me. She started talking about how I left cups everywhere and it made her insane. *Okay, okay,* I thought. I couldn't dispute any of that. That was all true. But the bitch couldn't have given me some *notice*? She had to try to move out while I was at *work* and not even tell me she was going? Even shitty landlords get notice when tenants are leaving. I was a friend of hers! I had thrown out my other roommate for her, my other roommate who may have been shady, but who always paid her rent. I felt my heart start to beat in my ears and my fists clench.

I walked into the kitchen, took a stack of her plates, and walked out my front door to the stairwell. The next thing I knew, I was chucking her plates one by one down the stairs. They shattered all over the place. I saw why Anthony had done it; it was satisfying to hear things crashing so loudly. She was screaming and trying to plead with me to stop. I ignored her and made trips back to the kitchen to get her glassware and anything else left, and proceeded to throw it all down the stairs. She was trying to block me and reason with me, but I just kept moving her out of the way and going about my business. Then I went to the bedroom and looked at her dresser. She begged me not to do anything to the furniture because it was her childhood furniture and it meant a lot to her. I was like, *oh really? Well out it goes.*

I took out each drawer and threw them all down the stairs. She was frantically trying to calm me down and I wasn't really listening, until I heard her ask me to please wait until her parents arrived with the truck to get her furniture. I stopped what I was doing. I said, "You want me to do you a *favor*? After what you just did to *me*? I should be nice enough to wait for your *parents* to get here?! Get the fuck out of my house. Give me your fucking keys." She handed over the keys, standing in the doorway. I took them and slammed the door in her face while she was telling me she forgot her glasses. I heard her go down the stairs crying. I became even more incensed that she had the nerve to try to get me to be fair. I felt like a fool for letting her move in.

After throwing all of her drawers down the stairs, I took the body of the dresser, which was light with no drawers in it, and threw that motherfucker down the stairs too. Then I went for her bed. I pulled that twin-sized mattress out on to the lawn in front of the apartment building in my peach lace bra and some men's boxers that I don't remember putting on. Then I dragged the box spring out, grunting and sweating. Cars were driving by, people were walking their dogs. Everyone was looking at me. The neighbors were coming outside because of all of the screaming and crashing and shit. I yelled, "What are *you* looking at?!" I was insane and didn't give a fuck.

An hour later, I was on the phone crying to someone when I heard a knock at my door. Still in my bra and boxers, I swung the door open to see Amelia's semi-hot Matt Dillon looking step dad. I yelled, "What do YOU want?!" and he said he was there to pick up her furniture. I hissed that everything was on the front lawn and he said there was nothing out there. I told him that wasn't my problem and slammed the door. I had so much adrenaline; I would have socked him straight in the head if he had knocked again.

When I think back on it, I think two things. One, I had an extreme reaction to the situation because my original family broke up in a similar swift, shocking manner, no notice, no warning, just bam! Surprise! Everything is changed; nothing is like you thought it was, you are out in the cold. You can't trust the people you thought you could trust. The second thing is that I wished I could just run to a mother. The fact that Amelia felt unsafe and uncomfortable and had the option to go "home" just *stung*. But the main reason for my behavior was, of course, that I had zero impulse control. I truly felt hurt and betrayed by Amelia and I felt completely justified in everything that I did. I didn't think about the times I had done the very same thing to people, just leaving with no notice. I only thought about how hurt I felt that she was being so sneaky and had hated living with me and waited until the last minute to tell me, leaving me screwed on rent.

I had been through worse things than that, but for some reason, I couldn't snap out of my sadness. I couldn't stop crying. I kept thinking *but she was normal...she was normal...normal people don't **do** things like that...*My thinking was very black and white- there was no gray. I had people sorted into boxes in my head: Good or Bad. Rich or Poor. Pretty or Average. Normal or Hollywood. The fact that Amelia had different feelings, thoughts, and wants completely screwed me up; it didn't fit into my boxes. My perceptions of reality were very demented and totally unbalanced. I felt so *confused*. I couldn't handle a betrayal, even a perceived one, by someone who was in the

"Good" box.

I had already bought the plane ticket to Florida, so I put on a baby t-shirt that said "Greedy Bitch," scraped my hair into an *I Dream of Jeannie* hairstyle, and got on the plane at LAX. It was warm and beautiful when I left. I forget who drove me to the airport. I just remember hearing the new Alanis Morissette song "Ironic."

Journal Entry 3/2/1996

It is probably risky to start writing things on a cocktail napkin, but I am on a plane flying to Florida with a bunch of strangers who could care less who I am or what I am writing. I stopped eating the pasta they served, because I can't let my stomach get full, it might bulge in some unseemly way. The other two items on my tray are also out of the question: a roll and crackers- too many carbs. The pasta was bad enough. There was also a little triangle of cheese wrapped in foil. Cheese is practically the root of all evil. I just stared at it. I did accept a Coke from the stewardess, knowing full well it contained 40 grams of sugar. I really only drink water, normally.

As we lifted off from LAX, I thought to myself: Fuck Los Angeles. I hope I never make it back. That place has made a fucking nut of me. It has been tearing me apart for twenty-two years. I thought to myself, if this plane goes down and I die...do I really even care? Not really. I am looking out the window, down on to something I have never seen before. Nothing. I am looking at nothing. I like it for once. There are no bank buildings or crowded patio eateries or assholes in shiny cars or packed freeways or shopping areas or salons or fitness clubs. Just fucking

nothing. A big area of space that no one has invested in,
because the land isn't in a prime spot.

Even though there is no one on either side of me or in front
of me, I am sucking in my stomach. I won't let it out. No
one even has a view of me. But I have a view. Why did I
eat the pasta?

Okay. Florida. I say Florida and not The Bahamas, because
we never *made it* to The Bahamas. Let me try and
summarize if I can. I went and met my friend in Fort
Lauderdale. We took a cab to the hotel and I saw the same
scenery passing by over and over and over; the cab driver
knew we didn't know where we were and he was trying to
keep us in the cab longer so the ride would cost more. I
took cabs to work every day (it was about $7 a day) so I
knew the deal. "STOP THE METER!" I yelled at him (you
knew I was going to yell that.) I just remember being out
in front of the hotel and pulling our luggage from the trunk
while my friend stood back watching in horror. I was
yelling at the guy and he was insisting I owed some
inflated amount. I gave him what I thought the ride was
worth and would give him no more. I was like, *fuck you;*
you aren't getting another penny and I just turned and
walked off while he yelled at me in Haitian.

We went out and got drunk off Lemon Drops and I faintly
recall jumping into a cop car to try and steal it. I started
pushing the buttons on the little computer. Then I
remember we went into a Denny's and no one would serve
us. We didn't understand why. After a half an hour of
watching other groups of kids get served, we got up to
walk out and everyone started clapping. I was puzzled.

The second night, we met some thugs and let them drive us to a club. They were total guidos in tight shirts. I recall getting to the door at some loud club and they were all excited that we were from California and they announced it over the DJ system. The guidos acted like our security detail and we walked around collecting free drinks. I gave a speech to my friend in the bathroom: if these guys tried taking us somewhere other than where we indicated, we needed to open the car doors at a stop light and jump out of the car and run; got it? I sucked on my drink and she nodded.

The next day, we were to board the ship for The Bahamas. It was springtime, so the weather was unpredictable. It started getting overcast and windy and the next thing we knew, it looked like a big crazy storm was coming in. They loaded up the ship with all of us suckers and kept it docked for an hour or two, hoping people would gamble. Then, they started to set sail in the storm. We were all sitting at tables eating, when the whole boat started rocking so violently that all of the glass came crashing off the tables and people started falling.

The boat rocked violently for several hours. It was really loud, which made it even scarier. We heard the sounds of the storm and people crying. You couldn't stand or you would fall. Everyone was lying on the floor, sea sick. We rolled one way. Then rolled the other way. Again and again and again. I saw the water splashing up over the side of the boat and thought, *This is it. This is the end. We will die here. This is completely out of control.* People were throwing up everywhere and bodies were just rolling, rolling, rolling along with everything that had fallen down to the floor. It was really scary for the first few hours and then after a while, my mind just became tired. I accepted that it was all over.

Somehow, they got us off that ship, twelve hours later. Everyone's luggage was soaking wet and sitting out in a big room. We were so tired and beat up we couldn't even talk. The company comped everyone's rooms for that weekend. I came back to L.A. afterward and told no one what happened. I couldn't even talk about it for several years.

Journal Entry 3/26/1996

It is hard to try and play the role of someone normal, someone who was not in a rough scene. It takes a lot of studying other people. I have to see what would scare a regular girl. I am so accustomed to such crazy things that I sometimes pretend to be shocked by things that I am not. I have seen a lot of wild things. It isn't ladylike. But it is me. It bothers me that I have to keep all of my past life to myself, but I guess that is how it supposed to be. It makes me feel like I fit in better with these rich, sheltered kids Charlie brings me around, but it is not me.

What did I have to hide? Well, I had to hide the fact that I walked around in a leather jacket and Motley Crue shirt, with a cigarette hanging out of my mouth at fifteen. I had to hide that I was cold, hard and hurting. I tried my hardest to hide that I was poor and that I didn't have a family home to go back to or parents to take me in if I wanted (let alone rich ones). I hid rapes, blackouts, violent fights, and trips to the mental hospital. I was determined to play off that I shit fluffy pink marabou and lived in a gingerbread house surrounded by sugar plum trees.

Journal Entry 3/27/1996

I remember when the joys of my life were handball, jelly shoes (not the chain link looking kind, but the kind that looked like ribs), mini-skirts with tights, puffy-sleeved shirts, anything with a rainbow on it, The Smurfs, *Jordache jeans (I wanted a pair and my mom bought me these crappy imitation ones instead), my "custom" lavender checkered Vans, my lavender Member's Only jacket,* The Karate Kid *and* The Goonies, *Duran Duran, Michael Jackson, My Cabbage Patch Kid with the little stitched belly button and butt crack, Willy Wonka, unicorns, Bubble Yum, Tinkerbell play makeup and perfume, my day-glo crayons, Tart n' Tinys, my Nerf ball, jump-roping and playing in the hose. I don't know what my joys are now. I don't want to be in this scary place I am in.*

But even scarier than the place I was in, was the place Birdie was in.

Thirteen

THE DECISION

I somehow caught on that Birdie had been seriously shooting heroin. Wait a minute...I am not sure what the difference is between shooting heroin and *seriously* shooting heroin; I guess it is pretty serious either way. I knew she did it on New Year's Eve. I also noticed that when she slept at my place after partying with Poppy that she couldn't wake up. Not even to go to the beach or to eat, two things she loved. I would try to wake her, but she was always in a deep, thick junkie sleep: eyes crusted shut, mouth open and drooling even with the sun hitting her in the eyes. But the thing that made me realize she wasn't just dabbling with this drug was when I found her "kit." It was a little tin box with a broken spoon, rubber bands, Band-Aids and a little travel size shampoo bottle. I opened up the little bottle and smelled bleach. I knew it was to clean her needles. I was sure there was a syringe in my trash can but didn't want to look. I was saddened, but not terribly surprised because she had always tried any drug put in front of her. I was with her the very first night she tried heroin, in Hollywood. I had hoped she wouldn't become addicted to the shit, but it looked like that was her new drug of choice. In all of her beauty, she was a secret heroin addict.

I wasn't sure what to do. Telling her parents was out. I had tried that years earlier and look where she ended up: worse. Threatening her and calling her a huge loser didn't work either. I had tried that back in Hollywood. There were parts of her personality that made me feel it was impossible to change her mind. First of all, she had no limit to the amount of drugs she would take. Second, she had no fear of being in danger. She would pop a ton of pills and drink until she fell over backwards in a tiny schoolgirl skirt. She was carried out of nightclubs, unconscious. She would get into any car, hang out with any stranger, and wake up where ever she ended up. She once called me at work and whispered that she didn't know what city she was in or where her purse was. She woke up in ambulances after overdosing on shit. Sometimes she ended up in the emergency room getting her stomach pumped.

She was in a really bad place. She was eventually blackballed from hanging out with my other friends, for one reason or another. Missy and Lisel were sick of baby-sitting her and making sure she didn't pass out or do something stupid. They were over it. I was avoiding going out with her myself, simply because it was too dangerous. I tried setting up things to do in the daytime instead of at night. One day I got her to go to the beach, like we used to, but she was suddenly uncomfortable being outside. When we got back to my apartment that evening, she stopped her car in my driveway and told me she had something to tell me. She took a deep breath and turned off the car. I thought she was going to finally fess up to her heroin use. I braced myself, staring at her profile while she looked straight ahead. She finally looked over at me and told me she had nothing to live for and that she didn't want to be alive any more.

She said, "All I have is my face."

I knit my brows. I thought back to our Hollywood days when she had deep, thick, bloody vertical scabs on her wrists from a previous suicide attempt. I remembered thinking that she must have really been trying to die, because everyone knows the vertical slices are the way to kill yourself, not the horizontal ones, which are for attention whores. Then I thought about a night out with Missy where Birdie got so drunk she started confessing that she wanted to kill herself. I felt incredibly disturbed. I realized that this was not some attention-grabbing thing she was pulling. This girl was planning on killing herself.

I was stunned at her reasoning as well. I was always under the impression that she was completely aware that she was using her looks to get her places. It was always kind of a joke between us, the thing on which we bonded. We always talked about how great we were because people fell all over themselves to be in our company. I was really shocked to find that it bothered her in actuality. I understood that it was a little depressing at times, I mean, sure- I thought about what it would be like for me if I were unattractive. Would people be so willing to help me find places to live? Pay for me to do so many things? Would I make as many tips? Would I have as many friends? I knew the answer was no. But deep, deep inside I knew I could be funny and entertaining and witty. Birdie didn't see anything else she had. She was still a beautiful little child inside, still a baby. She was a kid who had had ugly things happen to her at the hands of adults and who never saw justice. She was a kid who needed help. I looked into her pupils and saw anguish. I saw someone desperate, someone reckless. She didn't see anything else for herself. She saw nothing left to live for. She said if anything happened to her face she would have nothing, and she really believed that.

My mind started to scramble because I realized that I had a chance to talk this girl out of dying. The pressure of that made me turn into a total babbling fool. I told her she just needed to switch things up; stop sleeping all day and leaving the house only at night. I told her she was just getting depressed with the hours she kept and that the only people who were awake at those 4 a.m. afterhours clubs were shady people. I told her to get more sun in her life, be more active, I told her to try and hang around more normal of a crowd. She shook her head, she didn't want to do that, uh-uh, she didn't want to do that. I knew it was nearly impossible for her to suddenly join a crowd of kids her own age after all she had been through. I wasn't having an easy time of it myself, and I was one of the best actresses I knew. She would not have the patience to sit around with boring suburban kids and pretend to be interested in their lives. She would not be able to undo everything she had done to herself, everything she had seen, everything that had affected her.

I looked at her crying and I knew I couldn't save her. I

wasn't going to risk my own safety and sanity to try and save her from herself. Birdie and I had been in too many bad situations: car accidents, near rapes, too much alcohol/drug consumption- I still never knew what the hell would happen if I hung out with her. I did not feel safe with her. I had made a decision to get out of the Hollywood scene. I didn't *want* to try heroin when everyone else tried it. I wasn't exactly where I wanted to be, no. But I knew I didn't want to go backwards. I had to go on my own path. It was sad, but I couldn't turn back and try to drag someone with me who wouldn't do the work to get out.

I felt sick for her. I deeply hoped she would snap out of her current state of mind, but I knew it was time for me to get away from her. I would only go down with her.

I tried just staying around Charlie, but that proved to be a disaster too. She had become so controlling that it was exhausting me. I couldn't say no to her. I knew I was in debt to her because I had borrowed so many of her clothes and had let her drive me around at least twice a week if not three or four times a week for the past year. I knew I had not chipped in one dollar for gas or for any late night Jerry's Deli dinners. I knew I had mooched off her to no end. I had borrowed her perfumes, razors, and conditioners. I had eaten her food. I allowed her to cover me if any fee popped up anywhere. All of that mooching cost me my freedom. My head was spinning.

I started spending more time with my co-worker Allison. She lived with her parents in a beautiful house with little poodles tapping around inside. There were hundreds of blooming roses, dripping blossoms and twisting vines surrounding the grounds, which included a gazebo under an apple tree and a huge aqua blue pool in which we laid on rafts and drank Boonesfarm. Allison was my age and had grown up very similar to me in my younger years (teen years were a different story, of course.) She was from the Valley and knew many of the kids from my former neighborhood and the schools I had attended. She had been to Farrell's Ice Cream Parlor and Malibu Grand Prix and Devonshire Downs. She rode her bike and ate ten cent Now n' Laters after school, just as I had. It was very comforting to be around her.

She wasn't into elaborate makeup or dressing up and was amused at my dedication to both things. She was very smart and into more tomboy-ish things than I was, which I found very different and entertaining. She wanted to do tequila shots and eat crawfish in New Orleans. She went hiking, was into photography, and was an avid reader of books. I sometimes had to consult a frickin dictionary after talking to her because her vocabulary was so advanced. I finally just started saying "What does that mean?" right in the middle of when she was talking, and she would laugh. I had fun with her, learning about different ways of living life.

I remember the first night I took Allison out with my Hollywood girlfriends. She was waiting for me downstairs from my apartment. I was trying to make it down the stairs in heels and I slipped and ate shit down the last five stairs at the bottom. A few of my baby blue acrylic nails popped off while I was desperately trying to grab the railing. That was before we even got into the car. Then I had her drive me to the strip club to pick up Missy and Lisel so we could all go to The Room on Sunset.

We walked into the club to see Carmella on the stage, as beautiful and as golden as ever. I never saw my dancer friends or acquaintances actually *performing* at their jobs, so I didn't know the etiquette. I went up to the stage and tried to throw money at her and she looked pissed, but hugged me, topless, while her audience was watching. We all went out afterwards and danced and laughed and drank until the early hours of the morning. Cash was flying everywhere because the girls had just gotten off work and we were all exceedingly wild as the night went on. Missy kicked off her shoes in the street afterward, and Lisel and I were searching for them for a good twenty minutes (she always made it a point to kick off her damn shoes- even a brand new pair, it didn't matter. As soon as the night ended, the shoes came a'flyin, and we went a'searchin!) The next day I found a business card in my purse for some big sports agent, and I had to call Allison to ask her if he was cute- she said he wasn't.

Because we were so different, Allison and I started trading off weekends. When it was her weekend, she made me drink 40-ouncers and hang out at the Winnetka 6 drive-in movie theater with some gangsters or go to big house parties where huge fights broke out. When it was my turn, I glued eyelashes on her and put her in a dress and heels and brought her to the hipster places like the Chateau Marmont and ordered her martinis (and got someone else to pay for them.) They had a little plastic monkey (from that "Barrel of Monkeys" game) hanging off the side. She was fascinated at how I got into clubs. I would say, "Just wait right here with me." She would say "Here? We are like, in a dark corner of the parking lot." But within minutes, a doorman would be squinting over seas of people and motioning for us to come to the door. He would push people out of the way and let us cut in front of the lines. Instead of acting all cool about it, she made me feel good by being visibly impressed.

We were trying to steal bread from the kitchen at the Chateau Marmont one night, when we met some lawyer who brought us over some drinks. We went back to his little table and he was with the light-eyed guy from Milli Vanilli. We all got shitfaced together and had a grand old time. It wasn't until later that we found out Vanilli had pleaded no contest to three sexual assault charges a few months prior, and had just fled his court-appointed rehab. There was a $60,000 warrant out on his ass, which was recalled a few days later after the lawyer who bought us fifty million drinks told the judge that Vanilli left the rehab only to check into *another* rehab. (raises eyebrows)

Allison loved dancing to Abba, and one night as we were spinning around the dance floor, I threw my drink into the air behind me. The glass shattered on the dance floor, spraying onto a group of cholas with Sharpie-drawn eyebrows and crunchy hair. I was totally oblivious and not paying attention, but Allison was: she had to calm down a group of tough ass bitches who were pulling their hair back into ponytails and getting ready to whoop my motherfucking ass.

Another time that comes to mind is one day when we went through a McDonald's drive-thru and pulled over to eat the food. We watched a house catch on fire while eating our burgers! There were cars driving by and it was the middle of the day in a busy area, but no one seemed to notice. We thought, wait, this can't be real; someone would have called the fire station. I honestly don't remember *what* we were thinking; we may have been stoned. Nevertheless, this house caught on fire and then a huge tree went up in flames, while we sat there watching as if it were for our personal entertainment. I was dipping my McNuggets like a champ and feeling like I was at the Griffith Park Laserium watching a cool show.

Allison invited me to the beach one day. Her friend Angie came with us. They brought tons of beach toys, a CD player blasting the Mambo Kings and beach balls to throw. They had on shorts and tank tops and brought food. They were having a great time digging with shovels and making sand castles. I was in a metallic silver g-string bikini trying to tan my ass. I watched them laughing and playing and just being real and true and organic. It was strange to me, but it was beautiful. I forgot it existed. I didn't think it was possible to live like that. I hadn't thought to do that stuff in years. Fun had stopped being a part of the equation for me long before that. I only went to the beach to tan, in the skimpiest bikinis possible. It was strictly for vanity. Getting wasted was my only fun. I longed to laugh like that, play like that. I longed to not care what people thought. It was like there was a very small bud trying to break through the dirt to bloom. Allison was a very important part of my life for that reason. She showed me what life could be like.

As I went walking up in the hills that summer, I thought of something I had never thought of before. I dreamed of living in a small town. Of scrubbing off my makeup and settling down and just being in love. Having a family of my own. Of course I was terrified of even having a boyfriend, so I knew it would be something that would be hard for me. I was secretly still scared to death of men and usually avoided ever really knowing one or letting one really know me. I thought if someone really knew me, there was no way they could like me, let alone love me.

***

I came home from work one day that summer to find that my front door was open. Nothing looked as if it were missing, but a box of mine that contained my bank deposit coupons had been rifled through. I thought nothing of it, because I had lived with so many people through the years and there were always things out of place or people coming in and out.

A month or so later, I was charged $200.00 by my bank for a bad check. Someone had taken a deposit coupon of mine and wrote a fake check for $200.00 made out to me. They tried to deposit 100 of the dollars into my account and take the rest out in cash. The bank found that the check was bad and charged me for the entire $200.00. That was a lot of money for me; I was only making $150.00 a week at the time.

The first person I tried to blame was Poppy. Then, I blamed Amelia, whose belongings I had either smashed into a million pieces or thrown on the front lawn. I thought she was trying to get her money back for the broken items and furniture. Then I realized she wouldn't have the balls to break in my house and then forge my name on a check. She wasn't brave enough. I kept looking at the signature on the check and I was convinced it was none other than Missy.

I called her and promptly blamed her. She was appalled and totally insulted. She couldn't believe I thought she would need a measly $200.00 that bad. She was very hurt by it. Missy and I were never friends again. I never knew who took the check, but now I realize it was most likely the person who was on drugs and who had balls: Birdie. She would've done anything. She had committed several robberies of stores with her ex-boyfriend and had no shame.

Journal Entry 7/17/1996

The last time I truly got jacked, was when I was seven. I brought my little stash of Japanese goodness, Hello Kitty, into my second grade classroom and plopped down next to a girl named Tanya. Her hair was cut like a boy and she wore the same tan/peach/beige calico dress every day. She was dark- maybe American Indian or something and she always looked distressed. She didn't smile like the other children. She looked troubled. At any rate, we had these cardboard "pencil boxes" with our names on them. They were for school pencils, a ruler and one pink rubber eraser that smelled terrible. I thought it would be a grand idea to bring in shiny, bubble gum smelling, red and white Hello Kitty gingham-clad erasers with bows on them. Baby pink My Melody bunny pencils with balloons and hearts on them. Pastel blue Little Twin Star sticker books with puffy clouds, rounded stars and crescent moons. Tanya was salivating next to me, but I didn't think about it. I dumped the goods in and out of my dingy cardboard box over and over to look at them. She asked to see my bright pink jumbo pencil with a little tassel containing a teensy tiny baby set of pencils, hanging from the top of the eraser. I don't even think it was Hello Kitty- I am pretty sure I got the thing at Magic Mountain. I let her see it and quickly snatched it back.

*I went out to recess one day soon thereafter and returned to look at my stash of greatness. I noticed the cardboard box wasn't filled to the brim any more. It was about halfway down. I panicked and told the teacher I had been robbed! She asked me what was stolen and I was so flustered and upset that I didn't even know. I just knew the box was half empty. I took the box to the office, clunked it down on the reception desk, and announced that someone had robbed me. Again I was asked what was missing. I gave the genius answer, "I don't know, but this box was up to here and now it's only down to **here**." That shit didn't fly with the jaded office ladies at a school in the Valley. They sent me back to my class, probably thinking it served me right. It was not until I got home that I realized that the girl had stolen my big jumbo pencil! And she actually had the nerve to bring it to class about a month later and try to use it. I quickly told on her for stealing my shit and she got in trouble- big trouble. I just remember her eyes- they looked so sad. I probably looked like some lucky kid to her, one that had too much. And maybe I **was** lucky; maybe I **did** have too much.*

At that point, I was just exhausted. Starting with the Amelia thing and snowballing throughout the summer, I finally had a nervous breakdown. I called my Aunt Billie, who lived in Colorado. Actually, I think I may have written her a letter, because I remember opening the response letter. I was sitting on my makeup-stained couch in my apartment with the wood paneled walls and crying while I read it. I cried because my aunt and her family offered to let me move in with them in Colorado. I cried because I wanted to go, but I was scared to.

If I continued the way I was going, I was unsure of what

would become of me. I felt myself sinking. I felt myself losing control. I was living too fast, drinking too much, and getting into too many dangerous situations. I lived in a state of oblivion most of the time, and so did the girls around me. Everyone had their own problems they were trying not to face. The more I thought of just picking up and leaving town, the more I knew it was the only way to get out of the several ruts I was in. I didn't have many belongings; I had no career and no car. What was holding me back?

I made the decision: I was moving to Colorado. I gave my two-week notice at both of my jobs and packed up a box or two that my mother was nice enough to ship over there for me. My friends were sad and mostly insulted that I hadn't given them more notice. I didn't tell my Pao Pao friends until the day before I left (Jack was very offended and our friendship never recovered.) The reason I didn't tell them right away was because I didn't want them to talk me out of it. They would've laughed at me for weeks, reminding me there was no sparkles and glitter in Colorado. I was truly the least likely candidate for a resident of that state.

Journal Entry 7/27/1996

Today was average, except for the fact that neither Jack nor Allison spoke to me. I didn't give a fuck because I am leaving L.A. in one week. Maybe I will miss them, maybe I won't. Maybe I will miss Zuma Beach and Ventura Boulevard and ice blendeds at The Coffee Bean. Maybe I will long for Martinis at The Room or shots of Rumplemintz at The Century Club or to see the Boogie Knights perform on Sundays. Maybe I will miss laying out at Charlie's pool and and having sandwiches delivered in

95 degree weather, smelling suntan oil while she talks
endlessly on the phone. Maybe I will miss lunches with my
co-workers over at California Pizza Kitchen or Lite n'
Healthy Sushi, hot wind blowing our napkins into the blue
sky. Maybe I will miss being faded at the Golden China
Inn singing karaoke. Maybe I will miss Christmas
shopping at the Sherman Oaks Fashion Square, hustling
for decent gifts. Maybe I will miss Halloween costume
shopping in Hollywood at Playmates, dropping obscene
amounts of cash. I might miss hearing the crickets at night
while power walking up windy Valley Vista.

I hitched a ride with my grandmother and her angry new
husband Reginald, to Colorado. I felt like I was going to
throw up as we drove out of the Valley. I had to shut my
eyes. Was I doing the right thing? What the hell was I
getting myself into? I didn't care; I just wanted to take
action.

Fourteen

ASPEN

It was the summer of 1996. Everyone was afraid of Mad Cow Disease. A sheep was cloned. Madonna had recently announced she was pregnant with her trainer's kid. I remember hearing a lot of Toni Braxton, namely "You're Makin' Me High" and "Unbreak my Heart." I listened to George Michael's single "Fastlove" a lot. My nails were painted white. *Friends* was the big show and everyone wanted the "Rachel" haircut. My favorite movie that year was *Beautiful Girls*, starring Timothy Hutton and Natalie Portman. It showed a slow, snowy little town, somewhere I hoped to be.

And that is exactly where I was headed. My grandmother's new husband was driving 30 miles per hour in a large bucket of a car, degrading my grandmother the whole way there. We stopped to eat at a Denny's and he was just *terrible* to the waitress. She would have been a saint not to spit in his Super Bird. He left her a one-dollar tip after being totally demanding and rude. As we were leaving, I snuck a few extra dollars onto the table and he turned around and caught me. He was furious, like, *punch* someone furious. He called me a whore in the car. He said anyone who wore false eyelashes was a whore, plain and simple. I was like, okay, okay, I am a whore. Can we hurry up and go now, you old fuck? I thought he would dump me out in the desert and drive off. Anytime he had to ask something of me, he asked it through my grandmother, such as "Ask *her* if she would please stop *cracking* those sunflower seeds."

I was stuck out in the middle of nowhere, so I had to bite my tongue. We spent the night at a motel that looked as if it had housed many a serial killer, mid-spree. I think they paid for me to have my own room, because I remember being in one by myself and feeling relieved.

My grandmother called me once I got to Colorado and said it would be nice if I thanked Reginald for letting me drive with them. I bit my tongue while he got on the phone and I thanked him. He mumbled in a fake aristocratic accent, got off the phone, probably made himself a Southern Comfort on the rocks, and then beat my grandmother for the hell of it.

But that is jumping ahead. At this point in the story, I was there in the big old car, driving through the desert. Maybe it was Utah, I can't remember. We finally arrived in a little town in Colorado. My Aunt Billie lived in this big yellow house at the end of a cul de sac. There was a pasture behind her house that was full of cows! I was so stunned.

I remember feeling a little bit taken aback. There were mountains everywhere. There were pine trees. I mean, this was not a congested city full of crime and debauchery as I was accustomed to. They showed me to my room, which was in the basement. I loved it because there was a sunken down window. If I looked out of it, I could see up to the grass in the backyard. I liked it because it felt safe. I was very happy to be away from all of the bullshit I had created for myself. No turning my head away from drug deals, no roofies slipped in my drinks.

You had to be a natural beauty in Colorado because there wasn't much to help you out. I was very average without lots of makeup, so that is one of the first things I dealt with there, and it was much needed. I was painfully worried about my appearance living in California. I was convinced that everything rested on what I looked like. I required several products to keep myself looking groomed, none of which was available to me any longer. I wore certain makeup, used certain cleansers and lotions, and had to have my ultra-expensive hair products, all purchased from the beauty supply stores that dotted the Valley.

I had a little bit of it all to tide me over…but once that ran out I was going to have to make some changes and that terrified me. I realized I would eventually be faced with myself, stripped of all of my calculated glamour. There were no beauty supply stores in town. There weren't even any chain drug stores. Could I do this? Could I live in *Colorado*?

Journal Entry 8/10/1996

Jack and Allison were right. The only outdoor activity I

*have ever done was walk into a club. How will I adapt to
this unfashionable, outdoorsy, nature oriented
atmosphere? I am the complete and utter opposite. Where
will I fit in? I am renting a room from my Aunt Billie and
Uncle Ron for $500 a month, which includes food and
utilities, besides the phone. I doubt I will even use the
phone. There is no one I even want to call. I just want to
start over.*

After the shock of not having all of my beauty crutches
wore off, I settled into a beautiful realization for which I
was eternally, eternally grateful. Billie loved me. She
cared about me. She didn't just assume I was evil or
'watch her back' around me, despite a phone call from my
mother warning her to do so. She never withheld affection
from me. She trusted me. I had not experienced that in
several years. I am not saying I was trustworthy to my own
family back home as a teen. I wasn't. Maybe I deserved
that. But this time, someone was saying, hey, I heard all
the horror stories about you, and I don't care. I am going to
love you anyway and I am going to find out for myself
who you are and if you are to be trusted. I was astounded
that someone was giving me that chance.

It took me a little bit to get into a family mode. Billie, Ron
and their three kids (around 9, 7, and 3) all ate dinner at
the table together. They watched a family movie together
on Friday nights. The kids were like puppies, yipping
around excitedly, getting ready for birthdays, holidays,
school, and sleepovers.

It comforted me greatly to live in the house with them and
be a part of their family. Doing so saved me from
becoming a very jaded and bitter person. Now it was

different. I was living under a roof with my blood relatives. Kids that poked at me, smiled at me, admired me, and asked me tons of questions. An aunt that saved me from God knows what, just by taking an interest in me each day and talking to me on a deep level. Just talking to me at *all*. Getting to know me. Expressing love toward me.

I talked to her about the way my father was toward me as a pre-teen, something I hadn't yet discussed with anyone. She became furious. She wanted to kill him. I was stunned that someone was finally getting angry about what had happened to me; it validated it for me. It was the first time someone told me I had a right to be pissed. And not only that, but another piece of the puzzle was uncovered for me: Billie confided to me that my father had been sexual toward *her* as a young girl as well. *It wasn't just me. It wasn't in my head.*

I don't know if you can imagine what it is like being a child and dealing with your own father behaving in a pervy fashion toward you, but what happens is this: you don't want to believe it. You try not to think about it, you try to ignore it, you think, "maybe I just took that wrong" over and over. In order to go on, in order not to crumble, you must *not* let yourself acknowledge this fact. If you do, you will flee from the danger, and you *can't* flee, because you can't live on your own yet. You need the roof over your head, you need the clothes and the food and the school. You can't tell anyone, because that would require acknowledging it and you just *can't*. It is too disturbing. It is too vile. It is crushing, it is confusing, and it is the biggest mind-fuck you could ever endure. The person who is supposed to take care of you, the person who you should feel safe to run to, is actually the wolf, the devil, the person who you need the most protection from. It makes you go outside of your mind, outside of your body to survive. You are floating; floating with a lump in your throat and a pit in your stomach, trying to pretend you are normal, but feeling eternally dirty and tainted and ugly. There is a lot of moving things around in your mind. There are a lot of doors that are shut and never opened.

***

Billie's husband was friends with one of the local restaurant owners in town (there were precisely two restaurants) and he got me an interview. I got the job and started working at this pretty, log cabin-ish place, right on a river. The people were natural and kind, with the exception of one of Hugh Hefner's ex-girlfriends, who came in after bike riding with a bunch of friends and was very rude. The other exception was the restaurant owner's wife, who hated me and treated me horribly. It was almost comical how much of a shrew the woman was. It was clear she wanted me out of there. I hadn't seen a grown woman behave in such a way, except for in the movies. I wasn't terribly shocked at the cattiness, I had seen my share; but it was unexpected for it to be happening in such a wholesome place. She got so incorrigible that I ended up being fired or I quit- I think I quit but I can't remember. My nine-year-old cousin got a job there ten years later, and had the exact same problem with the exact same woman if you can believe it. I don't want to say she was jealous, but the only thing I can think of was that maybe she had a problem with her husband having affairs with the staff and she wanted to drive out the decent looking girls.

Since there were no other places hiring in town, I decided to look elsewhere. A few days later I got on a bus by myself and took the 20 minute or so ride into the next city, which happened to be Aspen, Colorado. I was wearing a baby blue eyelet sundress from Playmates of Hollywood, white patent leather sandals and tons of makeup.

It was the end of summer. I think it was September or maybe even October. I got off the bus at some sort of grand central station. The city was beautiful. It was, of course, an upscale ski resort full of international jet setters, but that wasn't what I loved, believe it or not. There were huge bright green mountains on all sides of me. There were Swiss chalet style hotels and buildings. There were old-fashioned lampposts, striped awnings and a lot of Victorian type architecture mixed with the sturdy brick buildings of a former mining town. It was so picturesque and scenic there. You couldn't tell what decade or country you were in. It was just timeless. I half expected some yodeling son of a bitch to zoom by me on a bobsled or the Von Trapps from *The Sound of Music* to some frolicking over the mountaintops in lederhosen. There were a ton of people around for some festival- it was either the Food and Wine Classic, the Playboy Jazz Festival, or something of that sort. There were a lot of festivals in the summer time.

I started walking toward the buildings, pretending I knew what I was doing. I was kind of excited. I thrived in that sort of situation, especially with a little booze down the old hatch. I found a bar called The Ute, went in and had a glass of wine for my nerves, and then set out to bat my eyelashes and get a job. I had no idea where anything was and I wasn't about to buy a map and look like a tourist. Banish the thought! I would have rather died.

I was buzzed and alone, but curious. I was happy to see

clothing stores that I recognized, but I knew I wouldn't be able to buy so much as a sock at any of them. There were Chanel and Christian Dior boutiques; Louis Vuitton and Bulgari stores...I was thinking I would be happy just seeing a Wet Seal, but no. There was not a lot of in between. You had to be a baller to even slightly enjoy yourself there. There were furriers, high-end jewelry stores, and art galleries. And if you wanted to eat, you were not eating at Applebee's my friend. You were eating at Matsuhisu Nobu's or Willow Creek at The Ritz.

After I finished my wine, I walked up Galena Street past a few stores and saw a total tourist restaurant; it was the only restaurant I recognized. It was a fucking wonder I even *found* a chain restaurant, because Aspen locals absolutely, fire breathingly (I know that is not a word) loathed any retail chain of any kind. There was a Gap on the corner and people were practically spitting on the sidewalk. I didn't understand what the problem was. I gathered that the places weren't special because there was more than one of them, but I didn't get the idea that they were considered "common" and low class. I found the chains comforting, but then again, I was also wearing glitter body lotion and baby blue nail polish.

I went into the chain restaurant and asked for a manager, prepared to flirt if it were a guy. Thankfully, it was a relatively young guy and by the time I got home, there was a message on the answering machine telling me to come in for training the next week. I later found out it was because I supposedly looked like a brunette Pamela Anderson, which is pretty much the look I was going for. Hey, I'm not claiming I was smart.

A week later, I started training at my new job. I was none too pleased with the uniform. It was hands down the ugliest uniform I ever wore in my life, the brown polyester slacks at Thrifty's notwithstanding. I had to wear this very loud tourist looking Hawaiian type shirt that featured tons of very bright primary colors splattered all over it- and you know how I feel about primary colors. It was SO hateful and humiliating. To top it off, the shirts were huge so I couldn't properly show off my proportions, which was something I considered important to my tips. I tried my damndest to show that I had a waist but it was nearly impossible. I decided to do the only logical thing a girl *could* do in that situation: wear a very short skirt. Yes, we could also wear pants, but who in their right mind would do *that*? So I was in this rainbow baggy shirt, a short skirt and some black tennis shoes. I was SO not chic.

I was geared up and ready to work, hoping the kids I worked with would be cool and fun. I enjoyed the nonstop upbeat music played on a loop in the restaurant; it was fun to dance around to when I was setting out the sugar caddies and salt and peppers. I thought, *now this is a nice pla-* but I was cut short. There was a strong smell of burning plastic in the kitchen, a smell I have only smelled once again in New York- and yes, that would be crack. Crack, as in crack cocaine. I forgot who told me, but I was like, *seriously dude?* Don't think that shit was a one-time occurrence either, like someone had a bad day back there making burgers. Those guys smoked crack all the time, despite the place being a family oriented tourist spot.

There was a beautiful upscale makeup place straight across the street. I would stand at the front window in my baggy rainbow colored shirt and stare at it like a starving child would a bakery or a candy store. I knew I could never afford anything inside but it didn't stop me from dreaming. The minimum wage in Colorado at that time was only around $2.00 an hour and I didn't exactly get the good sections at work. I was broke. I wore the cheapest, crappiest, thickest makeup you have ever seen. I looked downright spackled, like a bad sheet cake. I had on tons of glitter all of the time- don't ask me why- and frosty, silvery pink lip gloss that was very gooey at the corners of my mouth. I had my hair in two low ponytails and it was breaking off and thin from being out of my good hair products. I was pale already because there was nowhere to tan. I looked busted. I never had the right clothes for that town. I wore my work clothes on the bus to Aspen, with either a baby blue or a pale lavender puffy jacket over them. I usually had either a light pink, blue, or lavender headband on as well. I don't know why I always dressed like I was ten; it's probably because that was the last time I was happy. I even had a (whispers) *light blue, furry day planner to go with my nails* (hangs head in shame). I would pass by people with fresh, dewy skin and beautifully done highlights, wearing soft, buttery leather boots and fur jackets, getting into cream-colored Range Rovers and think to myself that they looked so dull and boring and needed to get with the program!

Halloween rolled around and I dressed up as a James Bond Girl. I don't know which one I was going for, I think I just wanted an excuse to wear white patent leather go go boots and huge false eyelashes with chalky pink lipstick (wait...I normally didn't need an occasion to wear such things). I found an emerald green sixties dress at a thrift store and stuck a toy gun in my boot and then went off with the one friend I had- a lesbian named Katie. We went to a club called The Tippler, which was at the base of one of the ski mountains. It was right next to a hotel called The Little Nell and was the closest thing to what I was used to. It played Top 40 pop and was a little flashier than the other local spots, although not by much.

A month or so later it started to snow in the daytime. It was dark and overcast. I went outside with a co-worker and we looked up into the sky and put out our tongues to catch snowflakes. The streets were dead. The ski season hadn't started yet and it was still just the locals. Twinkly lights lit up the brick buildings and the smell of cinnamon wafted from the bakery next door. The street looked flocked, like white velvet, and the old lampposts were lit up, releasing a dim glow. The sidewalks were heated, so the snow never blocked the way of passersby. I felt like I was on a movie set of some sort, it was so perfect.

When the ski season hit and the four mountains were open for skiing, the town was a madhouse. The wimps went to Buttermilk, which was the easiest of the mountains. That was where a lot of the kids I knew taught skiing. Most of the guys went to Snowmass Mountain on their days off because that was the only place that would allow snowboarding at the time. The hot shots in town skied the runs on Ajax, which was like, the coolest thing you could possibly do. There was a fourth mountain called Aspen Highlands, which was more intense than Buttermilk and less so than Ajax.

I didn't know how to ski and got a lot of shit for it. I knew I would be stupid to try because I didn't have health insurance and if I broke something I wouldn't be able to wait tables. I also couldn't afford the gear, not even to rent.

But the real reason was because I didn't have the true urge to get near a sport of any kind.

I stayed inside, watching the reports on Jon Benet Ramsey, a little girl who had been murdered in Boulder, which was nearby. It freaked me out that they couldn't figure out who did it. There were new shows out around then; MTV had a *Beavis and Butthead* spin-off called *Daria* that I watched. I also watched lots of the TV show version of *Clueless*.

I quickly became popular at work for being over the top and friendly. I thought I was fabulous and my co-workers got a kick out of it. I would interview everyone I worked with when I was bored and soon became the social director of the place, arranging parties and outings and activities. I was also the person who gave all of the girls makeovers. I didn't have much to work with in the way of supplies, but I had the skills to turn plain janes into glittery L.A. pole dancers.

As different kids came in for different shifts at work and I started to get to know everyone, I figured out who the partiers were. Basically, it was the night shift kids that went out drinking and the responsible older day shift people went home and knitted scarves or played Solitaire with themselves.

One time we all got wasted and went sledding on Aspen Mountain, a.k.a. "Ajax," in the dark, with bottles in our hands, singing that rap song "Tootsie Roll" at the top of our lungs. The mountain was not exactly best for drunken antics- it was no joke. It had a black diamond terrain and was like, 11,000 feet high or something- not that we got that far up. We nearly smashed into a snowmobile at the bottom, but rolled out of the way just in time. One of the Kennedys was killed on that mountain a year later, as was Sonny Bono the year after that. Both of them hit trees while skiing.

We all partied at the Tippler usually, but sometimes I was dragged other places, like The Smuggler and a place called Little Annie's that had red checkered table clothes and lots of people in flannel shirts drinking micro brews. Not my thing, chicken wing.

One day a girl at work showed me an ad in the *Aspen Times*: "Intern wanted for magazine." She and I had talked about our interests and she knew I was into journalism. After much encouragement from my aunt, I called the ad and they agreed to interview me. It was a magazine called *Aspen Magazine*. I took the bus to their offices one morning. They were on Durant Avenue, overlooking Aspen Mountain in a big log building with huge glass windows. I walked through the little lobby to see beautiful, stylish women with long legs and thick hair. They brought me into a little office that looked out onto some pine trees, and I met the chic, petite Asian woman who was to interview me. We talked a bit and I told her how much I had always loved writing and reading, and threw in a few funny stories about how out of place I was in Colorado. She seemed quite amused with me and liked my spark, but in the end she said she couldn't grant me the internship because the other candidates were college students and that was one of the requirements. I told her that someone either had it or they didn't- and I had it, college or no college.

I didn't even know what I *meant* by that, but it just came out. She smiled and said she admired me for believing in myself. She said she would keep me in mind if something opened up. I left disappointed, but not defeated, because I saw that she at least liked me somewhat.

Just being in those offices made my heart hurt. I wanted so badly to write, to be involved with the hustle and bustle of a magazine, to do something productive and creative. Then I thought, *well, that place is for kids with parents, an education and connections...not for someone like me. That kind of stuff doesn't happen to people like me.*

Birdie begged me to fly back to L.A. for New Year's Eve that year. She said her parents would pay for it, so I thought, shit, why not. When I got to the Denver airport, my flight was cancelled and the next one was eight hours later. I have never been so bored. I wrote on a notepad:

Journal Entry 12/29/1996

I am on an eight-hour layover in the Denver airport. I have surprised myself by not going crazy. I just read an entire book and then I bought this pad and a pencil, like a geek. Last night I had a total of two hours of sleep. It was an absolutely terrible night. First of all, I had to take a four hour bus ride to Denver. It shouldn't have taken that long, but the old bag of a bus driver started driving the wrong way and didn't realize it until we were an hour and a half out. She had to turn around and backtrack for an extra hour or so- with no apologies, just attitude. It made us very late. Then to top it off, the bitch said we were arriving in Detroit! She didn't know where the hell she was.

I sat next to this twenty-one-year-old boy on the bus, a

*college student. He was a terrible bore. I listened to his
unimpressive stories of dorm life for a good hour, while
nodding off. I was trying to be polite at first but after hours
of it I became delirious. I immediately stopped pretending
I was an intellectual like him when I broke a nail. I
couldn't help it; I went ballistic and blew my cover. I was
shrieking. I then decided to pull my big bag of beauty
supplies out of my baby blue carry on. He was peeking at
all my stuff so I handed each thing to him and told him
what it was for.*

*You should have heard this guy's stories. He said you had
to* **cherish** *red wine:*

"It's a **religious** *experience. You need to put on classical
music and breathe in the* **aroma** *of the wine and* **savor**
it...."

*I fucked up his whole speech by interrupting him when he
got to the pleasures of Merlot by saying that the only thing
I did with wine was pour the entire bottle into a huge cup,
get a straw, and try to pound it in two gulps. His
appreciation of French castles (oh please) and fine art
were equally phony and rehearsed. I am sure he probably
has some great internship somewhere, chosen over the
losers like me. It kills me!*

*His knowledge of the arts was completely ridiculous
because he didn't even know realism from surrealism. I
had to explain it to him. And it's not like I picked the
subject, either. It was even more funny when he tried
whipping out some cinematography knowledge because
then, broken nailed, bimbo here had to explain Mise-en-
scène to the bastard. Basically, this prissy airhead fucked*

up the school boy. It was entertaining. He said, "You rock my world!" and totally loved me and I even gave him my number so he could call me up and praise me some more. The bus was the least of it, though. Four hours on that crappy bus was heaven compared to the rest of the night. I am laughing right now because I am so miserable. I have been here since 7:30 a.m. It is now 2 p.m., and my flight is at 5:45 p.m. I had a rather crusty and leathery beef dip for lunch that has ended my addiction to beef dips once and for all. The little teenage girl with braces who served it to me gave me a free Coke.

*Moving on. Here is the rest of the story of last night: My friend of eight years, Justin Sandstrom, happens to live in Denver now. He picked me up at the bus station and we went to this distinguished, old fashioned sort of bar. We weren't very distinguished in our drink orders though- I ordered a Malibu Bay Breeze and he a White Russian. Tacky personified. But we aren't exactly scotch drinkers at twenty-three. We both actually looked rather preppy. Some strangers even came up and asked us where we shopped. I snapped, "We're not **from** here," rather rudely.*

Justin was asking me about my romantic life. We used to talk about that stuff all the time when we were teenagers and it was no big deal. But things have changed.

I planned to stay at Justin's house to save myself the price of a hotel room in Denver, as my flight was first thing in the morning. Now this is probably the one guy in the world who would never, ever try putting the moves on me. This was a guy I completely trusted and who restored my one iota of faith in men, just knowing he was alive.

When we got to his place, I became very uncomfortable. There was a lot of tension in the room. I agreed to smoke some pot with him- I was sure it would help the tension, but it didn't. It got worse. He got all quiet and was staring at me. I felt very uncomfortable and then became paranoid, because his best friend had killed himself in the adjacent room the year prior. It was a horrible thing for Justin to go through, but because I was stoned, my only thought was 'is this guy going to kill me? Maybe he is really a killer!' He kept moving closer and closer to me and I thought, 'this guy is going to pull out a machete and hack me to pieces and no one knows where the hell I am! No one would find me!'

Then he got really close to me and… started stroking my hair! He was trying to mack on me! I couldn't believe he thought I would go for it! This was a good friend of mine! Whom I thought respected me! I was so insulted. I got mad. Now, I know he is a guy and it is in their nature to try such things, and we girls are the ones that have to decline their advances or play dumb and pretend we didn't get the hint so as not to offend them. I am a pro at that one. But I was pissed that I had to worry about all of that with him, my friend!

*He was saying the sappiest shit I ever heard. It sounded like Pepe La Pew. He was saying I needed to be "loved right" and that I was a beautiful Italian woman and he was a beautiful Italian man (can you believe he said that?) and there we were together and he loved me. He **loved** me?! How dare he try to pull that shit with me. ME! Like I would fall for that. He had to go and say he **loved** me, to try to get me in bed? I was no longer afraid of that machete. If that motherfucker had one, I would have* *snatched it from his fucking hand and cold sliced his head off and then kicked it like a football off into the Rocky Mountains. Normally, he is the most sensitive and sweet person in the world. It was hard hearing him try to pull off that stuff. I was cringing for him. He was not good at it. I couldn't keep quiet any longer. I told him he was a bullshitter and that I deserved more than some stupid lines like that. I told him I was in no way ready to sleep with anyone, let alone him. I told him it was a mistake to have stayed at his house. I tried to go to sleep because I had to be up at 6:30, but he had me up until 4 a.m. trying to spew out his romantic, philosophical lines that he surely spent hours memorizing. It was one of the greatest disappointments I have had in my life. My father was one and my ex- boyfriend Jimmy was the other: finding out they were liars and not who they said they were. He was only a friend and not a family member or a love interest, but it was a great betrayal to me. There are very, very few males I trust. Along with some of my male childhood friends, I trusted Justin. I feel very let down, but not surprised.*

So anyway, he drove me to the airport this morning and I completely ignored him. When I got here, my flight was cancelled. I damn near lost it. So that is where I am now.

The L.A. trip was fun. Birdie and I went to a party at Sylvester Stallone's house from what I recall, his teenaged son Sage threw a rager.

I was getting settled back into my life at my aunt's when the phone rang. One of my little cousins said it was for me. I got on the phone to hear the voice of the woman who had interviewed me for the internship at *Aspen Magazine*. She said there was an opening and asked me if I were still interested.

I choked on my cranberry juice. They wanted me. *Me!*

I had no experience with magazines or offices in general. I just knew I loved writing. Was that enough? Could I pull it off without fucking the whole thing up?

Fifteen

TRUST FUND KIDS AND COCAINE

Walking through the doors of the *Aspen Magazine* offices made me beam with pride. I had a purpose. I was doing something productive. Something I actually *liked* doing that didn't involve the consumption of peppermint schnapps. They originally told me I needed to be in college to be an intern, but they made an exception for me. The other intern was a banking heiress named Ashley who went to Yale. That was the thing about Aspen, there were very few, if any, wanna-bes or posers, except for me. If you were in Aspen, you were loaded, plain and simple (unless you were one of the service people.) It was not a place where you could 'front' with any success. The people in Aspen were rich beyond rich, not just "I drive a leased Mercedes and rent a large house" rich, like the rich people in L.A.

Ashley was from a big New York family; her great, great

grandfather was right up there with J.P. Morgan. She rode horses in the Hamptons in the summer and spent winters there in Aspen. I went to her family's cabin sometimes and we hung out, laughed, and had a grand old time. She was down to earth and mellow, not at all heiressy- but it was clear she was very, very connected.

Anyway, I was the editorial assistant to the woman who had interviewed me, Audrey Wong. The first task she gave me was to go and gather updated information for the magazine's yearly restaurant guide. I went into each local restaurant by foot to talk to the managers, but they were never there, so I couldn't get the info I needed. I panicked as my deadline started approaching. I didn't want to screw up my first assignment! I decided to fax each restaurant their description from the previous year's issue and write, "This is the description of your restaurant we are going to run in the next issue. Please make corrections if needed." Lo and behold, they all responded via fax, scribbling and circling words on their descriptions, crossing out old phone numbers and adding others. Within a few days I had a stack of updated information. I put the guide together and met my first deadline. Whew!

After the restaurant guide, I did the Art Gallery guide, which was more of the same. It was sort of a tourist guide for the spring issue, for those who wanted to know which galleries to visit. Audrey had me update all of the contact info for the little blurbs. Then she gave me an assignment: I was to pick an art gallery that I liked and review it for the magazine. I was going to *write something* for the magazine? I started to sweat. Despite pulling some random info out of my ass on the bus with the boring college kid, I knew nothing of art or art galleries. I pictured them full of modern art, which I hated. I didn't think I would be able to find a gallery I actually truly *liked*, let alone write about one as if I were an expert.

I finally came across one called the Omnibus Gallery, which was located in a little brick mall sort of area. It featured rare vintage posters and advertisements. I was intrigued. I was an advertising freak- I made my own little ad agency as a kid. This gallery was right up my alley! I went in and interviewed the owner, who told me most of their posters were from the time period of the 1880's to 1939, when stone lithography was big and when advertising was at its most beautiful. Looking through the fluid, beautiful colored paper, I sighed with admiration. The advertising was art. Beautiful art. I went back to my desk at the office and wrote up a whole piece on the gallery without stopping. I gave it to my editor, who read it and looked up at me, smiling.

My story came out in the spring issue. I never felt so great. I saw it in the magazine racks at the market, next to magazines like *People*. It wasn't some little paper flier, it was a real, glossy, thick magazine with huge Gucci ads.

I learned something right about then. It was sloshing around with all of the alcohol in my body, but it was still there. I had spent many a night thinking, *It's not that easy...or someone like me can't do the things other people do...*Well, it WAS that easy. And I COULD do the things other people did. I was supposed to go for it, even if I wasn't qualified, even if someone said I couldn't do it. I was supposed to at least try.

I had another writing assignment that showed up in that

issue. It was a 'then and now' piece on a couple that owned a place in Aspen called Trentaz Ranch, which later became the luxury area known as Starwood. I called the elderly couple from my room down in the basement at Billie's and interviewed them, writing down their answers on a piece of notebook paper. They reminisced about the early days of the ranch, when they sold eggs for 19 cents and worked the land themselves. They talked about how crowded Aspen had become and how they were now running into former presidents when they went back to town. I took my notebook paper to work, shaped it into a story, and gave it to Audrey. She was impressed that I completed it so quickly and ran the piece. I have to add a little tidbit here because it is kind of crazy: Starwood later became the location of the most expensive real estate in U.S. history, and possibly in the world, when a ranch built by a Saudi prince went on the market for $135 million dollars. A lawsuit was later filed, alleging that the prince had built the property with frickin bribery money taken from a British defense company for fighter-jet sales to his country.

Okay, so, the magazine wasn't paying me and I didn't mind, but my lack of funds sometimes put me in uncomfortable situations. I would often turn down lunch dates because I didn't have money and I felt ashamed and embarrassed of my lack of table manners. I was also suddenly embarrassed of my shoes and clothes- they were almost falling apart. The women around me were all very well groomed; I certainly stood out as shabby. All I had in my closet were the club clothes I had purchased in California; I had never thought to buy anything classy. What worked in a dark, crowded nightclub, did not look good in an upscale resort town, and most definitely did not look good in an office setting. I tried to get some office clothes on my meager waitress salary, but I couldn't get much. I remember wearing this pleather jacket with no lining in it- it surely still had some sweat droppings on it from some ten-year-old Thai sweatshop workers.

I looked like shit, but I had drive. I was truly interested in my job. I volunteered to run errands for the art department, to see how things worked. The guy in charge of the layout of the magazine let me watch him one day, arranging pages on his drafting board. I also helped the advertising department quite a bit, so I could get a peek into that world, but I found that it was purely sales. They sold ad space and schmoozed, period.

I still worked at my waitress job on the other days of the week. I mostly hung with a petite red-head named Samantha, who had transferred from the Seattle location. There was a girl named Jessie, who was a bit of a tomboy and who liked the band 311. She practically had a penis. There was a gay guy named Rich, who always did a big black mama impression: "Come to mama **bay**yyybie- come put yer head in mah **bus**soms." There was a total nut named Will Bensen who amused the shit out of me with his outrageous lies, like for instance, that he once worked for the CIA as a sharpshooter. He loved Charles Bukowski and was always saying funny things, but he was a mess.

There were only three guys at work who we considered even semi-hot. There was Jason, who was only cute from certain angles and on certain days. Have you ever known people like that? Anyway, he was kind of a granola head who had feathered hair and was from San Francisco. He had a weak chin and a lame laugh. Samantha was always into him and if I were really bored, I would flirt with him myself. Then there was Mark, who was a rich, young kid from Manhattan. He had green eyes; a flat, wide face and curly, longish brown hair that he pulled back. It was not a cute hairstyle at all, but he was cocky and smart, so it raised the level of his attractiveness. I liked bantering with him. Two new kids named Dax and Harlan started working there during ski season and I had a crush on Harlan, even though he was a little young, because he was tall and had dimples. We also worked with a really loud, obnoxious Texan named Laura Lynn, who used to get drunk and say HAY Y'ALL so loud, it could shatter glass on the other side of the country.

Most of the kids I worked with lived in the "employee housing" in Aspen, which was really just a cool apartment complex that looked like log cabin motels. It was the shit! It was called The Marrolt and everyone made fun of it, but I thought it was plain awesome. The buses would pass by there after the clubs closed and dump everyone off. What more could you ask for? I spent so many nights at The Marrolt, partying from room to room that I ended up moving my clothes into Samantha's apartment. She lived with two other girls, so it was crowded with me there too. We would work, go back to the apartment, do tons of shots of peppermint schnapps while getting ready, then stumble out into the snow to get on the free bus to the clubs.

We all hung at The Tippler or this place called Maxfield's. It was the bar in the Grand Aspen Hotel, which was also at the base of the skiing mountain Ajax. The place was always playing Irish drinking songs and was considered a dump compared to The Little Nell and the Ritz Carlton. It had foosball tables and ten-cent chicken wings; it was exactly the sort of place where broke waiters could drink beers. Believe me, I wish I could be writing about the inner workings of The Caribou Club, but I didn't work up to that spot in the year I was there. I was definitely on the wrong track with my boisterous antics and cheap, flashy wardrobe.

Caribou was this private club that was members only- it was like, $500 dollars a week for a membership or something like that. Someone told me you could get a lifetime membership for twenty grand, which made me choke on my Power Bar. I tried to ask around to find out who went there, but all I could get out of people was Bill Clinton, Goldie Hawn and Diana Ross, which is good enough, I guess. I was also intrigued to hear that there was a special red phone inside that had a direct connection to the Aspen airport, so you could call for your private jet. Fancy Shmancy, huh?

I actually did get to go inside one time, to bring some copies of Aspen Magazine to someone in the middle of the day, when there was no one there. The entrance was an unmarked mahogany and brass door, and once I got inside I had to go down a big long staircase that led down into a room painted in British racing green with dark moulding trim. It was a pretty masculine looking place. There was a wine cellar and a bunch of landscape artwork on the walls, stuffed chairs and a big fireplace.

Okay, so, back to my story. A bunch of hotties came into town for the ski season, mostly rich kids on holiday. Samantha and I competed for the hottest ones and we hooked up with a few. We battled for this one blond model, who I won. I had this crazy liaison with him, then he left, went back to the party we were at, and hooked up with *her*. She tried bragging to me later and I said, "Hope you had him brush his teeth first…" She was like, "What? I'm gonna kill you!" We had quite a laugh about that one.

Another night I caught a guy drugging our drinks with the date-rape drug GHB. (So much for me moving somewhere where I was to avoid trouble.) We were already a few drinks deep when I caught the guy dumping some stuff in my drink. I just remember it was champagne with Chambord on top- and then a little roofies on the side I guess. I remember coming back to the Marrolt with a glow necklace on and feeling crazy. I didn't black out or get raped or anything, thankfully.

I loved Samantha to death, but she wasn't like the girls I was used to. Then one day this golden blonde Barbie walked into my work in slow motion. She was a new employee. Her name was Hope Harrington and she had an upturned nose, frosty pink lipstick, piercing blue eyes, golden skin, golden hair, and a lavender clip holding her hair up. She has fit and tiny and girly. I clutched my heart and sighed. Finally. A girly girl!

Hope and I became inseparable. She drove a silver BMW, she played rap music and Prince, she wore lots of pastels and she had money. *I was in heaven.* I wanted to snuggle up to her like a cashmere throw. I had missed her type. She didn't live in the Marrolt like the others. She had a big cabin in the hills of Aspen. I felt all tingly inside because I was such a gold-digger and looks-digger. Even for friends! Geez. I was thrilled to have found her and was ready to climb up into another level of the social circle with her. I wanted into the Caribou Club! I had PLANS!

So I started hanging out with Hope. She had been dating the son of a very famous and wealthy international businessman whose name I will not mention. (By the way, I know I am being *such* an annoying name dropper in this book, but I want to write what actually happened- forgive me!) She was not only beautiful, rich, and fun, but she 1) always gave me pills and vodka, 2) drove me around, 3) let me wear her pink clothes and 4) let me sleep in her big bed instead of spooning with three girls in a twin bed in the Marrolt. Got it?

So I was moseying along nice and content, when I realized that she was doing coke. I noticed her scoring it and doing lots of lines. I thought, *whatever. I am in Aspen.* Then I saw that she started *smoking* the coke and I thought...*wow. She doesn't look like the type that smokes coke.* But I ignored it and threw back more drinks. One night she shoved some makeup at me and asked me to cover up the sores on her legs and arms. I squinted and looked closer- she had tons of open wounds. Whoa. Okay, smoking coke must give you open wounds, note to self.

I started to notice that her eyes were dead- there was nothing behind them. There was no soul, no emotion, no *nothing*. She was shut off completely. I was so wrapped up in her looks and wealth that I had never looked before.

I remember that on the way to The Ritz one night, Hope stopped at the jewelry store she worked at in the evenings. She unlocked it, took some huge rings and bracelets in the dark, then came back out to the car, and gave me a huge cocktail ring to wear that cost who knows how much. I was hammered, wearing tons of jewels that weren't mine, in the Ritz Carlton drinking for free.

It was so crazy all of the time, I swear, every single night I would be thinking, *how did I get here?* I never got a chance to sit and regroup; I was always going, going, going. Partying, writing for the magazine, going back and forth on buses; it was just insane.

And that, my friends, was around the time I really started to see what Aspen was all about. (sighs). Okay...how do I start here? So I am in Aspen, initially partying with these average kids who were cool and drank and this and that. Yes, the guys in the kitchen smoked crack and yes, the line cook dealt coke - but I mean- there was always *one* drug dealer wherever I went- I didn't think it odd. And then I met Hope and I thought...*okay, so she parties a lot.*

It always seems to be the big joke that there is a lot of coke in Aspen, but it is really true. In the bars, they take big measures in the bathrooms. Some places drill holes on the little shelf where you put your purse, or spread it with Vaseline, so people won't lay out lines. This is a tiny town we are talking about. Even today, they are still having the same problems: They just found a large amount of cocaine in the basement at the Wheeler Opera House. A drug deal was intercepted in the J-Bar in the Hotel Jerome. Police just busted an Aspen car wash cocaine ring. Coke was and is downright rampant in that city. Drugs were everywhere when I was there, and the rich kids were consuming them with fervor.

Hope introduced me to a guy who was tall and semi-cute. When I first saw him face to face, I thought, *not hot,* but then he started talking. Let's just say his name was Trust Fund Kid. He was young, about twenty (I was twenty-three), unimpressed and cocky. Wasn't afraid of me at all.

He grabbed my arm and said, "Come on, you're coming with *me*," and I laughed. I was like "I can't, I have to work in the morning and I don't have any clothes with me," (that was my only reason?) He said, "I will buy you all new clothes in the morning," and he wasn't kidding. I was intrigued with his cockiness but also thought, *I do need some new clothes! Bring it!*

Trust Fund Kid was the son of a prominent Aspen socialite. I never asked him about money, but he did blurt during an argument one time, "Do you know how much *money* is coming to me when I turn twenty-five?!!?" He wouldn't be twenty-five for another five years, so he dealt coke to the locals in the meantime. This included his mother and stepfather, which always startled me. When I met his mother, she asked me if I wanted a bump of coke! I told her I didn't do drugs but didn't mind if she did. Trust Fund Kid lived with them until he ripped them off on a coke deal and they threw him out of their house.

Since I was a total idiot, I was highly entertained and excited by his lifestyle and most of all his attitude. He would walk into a market, snatch a bag from the checkout stand, walk through the place without blinking, fill the bag with whatever he wanted, and walk out the door without paying for anything. He was nuts. I thought it was hot. I quickly fell for the guy and I felt my heart flying off. I guess the blatant stealing of groceries and the dealing of drugs made my heart swoon, shit, I don't know.

What I *didn't* find hot, was the fact that Trust Fund Kid also smoked cocaine. Most of the kids from Aspen did. They were the richest kids I had ever seen in my life and they were behaving like total crackheads in the ghetto!

I quit the restaurant job around that time because one of the cooks, some big red headed guy, started cursing me out really hard and screaming in my face and it scared me really bad. I quit on the spot. I got a job at the only pharmacy in town, Carl's Pharmacy, which looked like an Austrian brauhaus. Let me tell you about it real quick and I will get back to the craziness. I liked working there because they had Estee Lauder cosmetics (Estee Lauder herself had a house in town and was there quite often with her family.) They also sold false eyelashes, so I was in heaven. It was sort of a mom and pop store, but people like Sally Field would come in, or Hunter Thompson's handlers (he was a recluse and never came out by himself) It was like, the town store.

On Sundays, everyone would line up to get their papers, because we had *The New York Times* shipped in- people went berserk for it. We also had *The Wall Street Journal* and *Barron's*. People needed their papers and would get irate when they had to wait until I marked them off on the innovative system that consisted of 3X5 recipe cards, a little recipe box and a gnawed-down pencil.

I have to tell you about my co-workers, just so you can get a feeling for the place. I worked with a girl named Mindy who was totally nutso and poorly groomed. She was in need of a good bra, some good laundry soap and some decent shampoo. She wore glasses that she always pushed up on her nose. There was a rich girl named Bianca, who was deathly pale and skeletally thin with damaged, dyed red hair. She said she had irritable bowel syndrome. I must've heard about her bowels a thousand and one times. She was dating the boss and got away with never coming in. There was a hot snowboarder named Chad who looked a tiny bit Asian but had dark skin and some blond in his hair. He couldn't be bothered with dating me, which made me have a crush on him. I would brag about how great it was in L.A. and he would shoot me down, saying things like "Well if it's so *great* there, why don't you go *back* already?" I was always left with my mouth hanging open. He wanted nothing to do with me. It was great. He always went out for cigarette breaks and wanted everyone to cover the counter for him.

There was Pauline who worked behind the make up counter, who once gave me a brand new compact of Estee Lauder Lucidity pressed powder when I dropped mine after spending half of a dwindled paycheck on it. She was smart and calm, with curly red hair and pale skin. There was Patty, who was very neurotic. She always wore long flowered dresses, had a short pageboy haircut, and seemed like she would burst into tears on some days. There was a tall blond hottie named Hans who worked in the liquor store whom we didn't see much of because he was on the other side of the wall. He was one of those guys who made full on eye contact with you when he smiled at you, which made my underwear twist into a pretzel and my feet flutter up like a helicopter. Finally, there was a smart, capable brunette named Elizabeth from Cape Cod Massachusetts, who thought I was the most awesome thing in the world. She got a huge kick out of me, always laughed at my jokes and thought I was great. I loved her for loving me. She was pale, had shoulder length black hair and light eyes and wore lots of L. L. Bean, Eddie Bauer and The North Face clothing. She would tell me stories of her fiancé, Tip. We laughed together quite a bit. She was like a great older sister.

Alright, back to the story. It was around March of 1997 when a few things happened that bothered young adults like me. The first thing was that a rap artist known as Notorious B.I.G. (don't know what that ever stood for) was shot and killed back in L.A. His music was what we were dancing to in the clubs prior to my move to Colorado. I was disturbed. I knew it was retaliation for the Tupac Shakur murder about six months earlier in Vegas and I was just really bummed. Then there was a mass suicide by some cult called Heaven's Gate. They all wore black sneakers and laid down on twin beds after poisoning themselves; carrying a five dollar bill and three quarters in each of their pockets- the whole thing messed with my head and upset me. I also had additional anger when I wrote my mother a letter about what I thought my father may have done to me. It was at that time when I received a response from her telling me that she had *suspected* my father of being sexually inappropriate with me. I was full of rage that she never asked me through all of my horrible, dreadful teen years if I needed help, if I were okay, if I were in danger.

What I did when things upset me was get drunk, so I made sure to go out every night. Now I could have chosen to go to church or see a counselor, but I chose to get wasted. I always got quite drunk in the clubs because I took to walking up to any full drink I saw in front of me and drinking it, no matter whose it was. I would also grab any coat I saw laying around, put it on, and walk outside into the snow. I often went to the Popcorn Wagon on Mill Street with my friends at 2 a.m. It was literally a big red wagon that housed a guy inside who made these spinach and cheese crepes that I loved. I don't know who the F paid for my food, I just know it wasn't me because I never had any money. I remember being so hungry that I could've eaten out of a dumpster.

I hate writing this, because I am still mad at myself, but...I quickly lost sight of Billie and her family. I had this person who cared about me, who defended me, who loved me, and I gave up strengthening that relationship and the relationship with her kids, so I could party more. I had a chance to change my life and clean myself up and move in a different direction, but I was too intrigued with and tempted by my new surroundings. I went back to her house every week or so to do laundry or get more clothes. I was such an asshole (sigh). I would ask Billie to give me a manicure and then take off again for a few weeks.

One night, Trust Fund Kid introduced me to his best friend, who lived in Europe part time. His family was loaded and he had a twelve million dollar trust fund waiting for him. For high school graduation, his father had ordered him ten call girls, lined them up, and let him choose who he wanted to sleep with, as a gift. I was like... *uh...wow.* There's a great dad, huh?

And speaking of call girls, I was at Club Freedom with TFK a few days later and I saw two young blonde girls on the attack. My heart sank and I felt weird. I knew straight away that they were hookers and that they would end up with him.

The two girls checked in with an overweight, balding man sitting at the bar. I had never seen a pimp before. Most hookers I knew worked for themselves or escort companies, but not these two girls. The fat pimp ordered them drinks and was very mean to them. It looked scary.

They were so young. They had to go everywhere with this big fat guy and do whatever he said. Part of me wanted to help them escape this man. He just seemed dangerous.

Trust Fund Kid walked in and I saw them eyeball him as their next mark. I went over to them and begged them not to get with him. If you can believe it, I said, "I know you have to make money and everything, but please, please...not him." And they were as sweet as pie: "Honey of *course*! Don't *worry*!" I even stuck around with a rock in my stomach, hoping to block it. But once I left, TFK gave coke to the pimp in exchange for an evening with the girls. He was honest about it the next day and told me what happened. I started crying and promptly dumped him- only to forgive him a week later.

One night I skipped out on going for margaritas with the work kids to hang out at The Marrolt with TFK. He said something rude to me and I punched him straight in the mouth. He stormed out the front door just as we heard a huge crash. He went to see what it was and came back into the apartment and threw up. There had been a terrible car crash- someone drove off the cliff above The Marrolt and landed in the apartments across the courtyard, smashing right through the building. Minutes later, hydraulic rescue tools were extracting someone out of the mangled car. There were dead bodies and blood- I didn't want to look. I was terrified. Samantha ran in the apartment and said it was our co-workers in the car.

It ended up being our buddies Dax and Harlan and two other kids who we had hung out with a few days prior. Dax had been driving and lost control of the car. He and one of the other kids survived, but the second guy and

Harlan did not make it. They were killed instantly. I think the worst thing I have ever seen was Harlan's funeral. Dax stood over his open casket, looking down at his best friend since grade school. I couldn't even look at them. Harlan's head was put back together for the viewing and Dax had part of his head shaved from a surgery. He stood up and apologized to everyone, to Harlan's family, taking full responsibility for killing him. I was just…I don't even have words for how heavy it was.

Things were becoming harder for me because I was heartbroken over Trust Fund Kid almost every day. I couldn't think straight. The heartbreak would end with some bold move on his part, like grabbing me in the rain in the middle of traffic and kissing me like a movie star. One time I didn't have the appropriate shoes for something and I just remember him saying, "Who *cares*? I don't give a fuck- I will take off my shoes and go all the way over there in my *socks*!" and he kicked his shoes high into the air, without even glancing as to where they were going to land. I remember that one shoe sunk into a bush and the other went out of sight somewhere. He picked me up, threw me over his shoulder, and walked to wherever we were going in his socks, never even turning back for his shoes. It thrilled me. I admired people who didn't give a fuck, and this guy certainly didn't. I was a sucker. A total idiot, allowing things to occur that I would have never normally accepted. I was in some sort of a trance.

When I was working at Carl's Pharmacy, he would bust through the doors, nod his head at me, walk straight to the cigarettes, grab some and stuff them in his pocket. Then he would go steal some lotion, snacks and whatever else he wanted and walk out of the store. He would not even *attempt* to hide what he was doing or even look up. The man back in the pharmacy, who had been there for forty years or something, stopped even scolding me for TFK's thieving. He quietly marked all of the items on a piece of paper and took them out of my paycheck, which would leave me with these measly $60 dollar paychecks. And it got worse- I would hand over the 60 bucks for TFK to pay his phone bills at the Tyrolean Lodge down the street, which was this Swiss themed hotel in which he would sit around and smoke coke. I would walk over there after work and he would grab my compact and stuff a baggie of drugs inside and tell me to hold it until later because he had a deal to do. I was partially thrilled and partially pissed.

Things were getting insane in town. Hope was getting sicker and sicker and more spun on coke, and I was exhausted from keeping up with her and the others. I was completely screwing up my internship. I had to write a piece on the bar at the Ritz I believe it was- or maybe it was the Hotel Jerome or The Little Nell, I don't remember, but it was about the new tequilas that were coming out. They also trusted me to do a restaurant review, in which I had to eat Carpaccio, which is completely raw meat. I had my little tape recorder with me and was buzzed while trying to do the review. The chef and the manager were treating me like royalty, trying to get a good write up, but I nearly barfed. My editor read my review and wouldn't run it.

I partied harder and harder and stayed up later and later, soon becoming so burnt out that I could hardly stand up straight. As spring became summer, I decided I needed to move on. I still kick myself for leaving that magazine and my wonderful aunt, but that's what I did. I thought that I would have more journalistic opportunities in a big city, and wanted to try getting an internship back in California. Or that is what I told people at least. The truth was, that I was getting too wrapped up in Trust Fund Kid and his world of drug dealing, and I saw bad things for my future if I stuck around even another month.

I didn't want to tell him I was leaving for good, so I told him that I was going to visit L.A. and would come back in a few weeks. My heart was beating wildly because I knew I would never see him again.

Samantha agreed to drive me all the way back to L.A. We stopped and bought the new Spice Girls single "Say You'll be There" and played it loudly, screaming and whooping and being all around idiotic. Samantha had a bunch of coke in order to do the night driving- it was totally acceptable in our town and our crowd so I wasn't shocked. But I was shocked at *myself*: I wanted to try some

Now folks, I will be the first to say I was a complete moron (sigh). But I am here to tell you the facts. We went into this little mini-mart gas station type of place in the middle of nowhere. There was a big huge cartoon of a beaver or chipmunk on the side of the store. The sun was kind of about to set so everything was really bright and golden. It was hot out- we were wearing tank tops and shorts, with our hair in clips. Samantha and I walked into the bathroom and into a stall. She chopped up some lines on the back of the germ infested toilet tank with her ID. She rolled up a dollar bill and snorted one of the lines. It disappeared into her nose and she laughed. She handed me the dollar bill. *What the hell*, I thought. So what if I had made it through my entire duration in Hollywood without doing drugs. So what if I had just made it through living in *Aspen* and managed not to do drugs. I was curious. I felt that there would be no way I could continue on with the drug once I got back to L.A. because I would not be exposed to it. I thought this would be the perfect time to try it. It would be just this once...

I bent down and put the dollar bill on the porcelain tank. I think I only snorted half of the line, because I was scared I would get too high. I felt it hit my mucous membranes. I stood back up and looked around the stall. It didn't take long to feel completely euphoric. I am talking rainbows shooting out my ass. I felt like I was going to burst with a combination of contentness, happiness, joy, and self-confidence. I also felt brave. Really brave. I wanted to do something crazy. I looked at Samantha and said, "Let's rob a liquor store," and I was dead serious. I felt like I was gorgeous, funny, witty, smart, sexy, and unstoppable. I felt like nothing could hurt me. I felt superior. I felt sort of like a superhero.

In a way, I am glad I tried coke. It made me think differently. I no longer assume someone wouldn't do something because it's too crazy. Often I would think, "Oh, no one will try to break in my car, it's the daytime on a busy street." Wrong. A drug addict thinks it's a great idea. *Everything* sounds like an awesome idea, even the very *worst* things. So basically, it taught me that there are people walking around who don't apply regular common sense to their actions. Lots of people. It made me see how someone could strip in front of strangers, how someone could become a criminal. It was the glimpse into the mind of a bad guy.

But at the time, it was just plain euphoria and all I could think about was doing it again. I wanted to feel like that for the rest of my life. I couldn't remember ever, ever feeling that good and confident and thrilled. I begged Samantha to find us more and she said there was nowhere she knew of to get more. We were in the middle of nowhere. I could see how someone would go to crazy lengths to get drug money, because that is what I felt like too. I don't know if it was just really good Aspen coke, or it was because it was my very first "high." But I know I loved it.

Was I going to become a drug addict?

Sixteen

THE FUNERAL

I learned something from my stay in Aspen. I learned that my problems were not the fault of the town I was living in, nor the people I was hanging out with. They weren't the fault of the Sunset Strip Scene or glam rockers. They weren't the fault of the L.A. club scene, or rich California kids. They weren't the fault of the town of Aspen and the trust fund kids. They weren't the fault of my family, whom I blamed all my situations on, deep inside. They were *my* fault. My behavior was not changing. No matter where I went, it was coming with me.

It was August of 1997, and I was back in Los Angeles, living with Charlie. We were living in a powder pink condo with a fluffy white Persian cat. There was a glittered star on each of our bedroom doors, like they were dressing rooms. My room was powder blue and full of my comfort items: Barbies, My Little Ponies and Hello Kitty shit.

I took another waitress job, a place that had a huge menu. I thought I would never learn the thing. Little did I know, the menu was nothing compared to many of the a-holes I would have to deal with. And some days the people were nice, but the place was run so badly, it made the experience crappy for everyone involved. Food would be hot and ready to be brought out to the tables, but there would be no clean silverware. So what do you do? Well, when you are running around like a maniac, you don't have time to think- you just act. We were all slamming into each other with fistfuls of silverware, running them under cold water in the sinks and wiping them dry with our little hand towels.

People would want coffee, but there were no clean coffee cups. They would want soup on a rainy day, but guess what wasn't clean? Soup bowls and soup spoons. Sometimes the dishwasher was just backed up, but most of the time it was because they refused to order more of these supplies.

There were also times when Immigration and Naturalization Services, otherwise known as INS, would do a sweep and wipe out half of our staff, because they were mostly illegal aliens from Mexico. They would take the dishwashing guy and the pizza guy, and a bunch of bus boys. One time they took the pizza guy back across the border, so we didn't have pizzas, which I had to explain to a table of business guys. One of the guys said, "Is that *my* problem? I want *pizza*." I ran to the back to make one, crashing into other waiters who were throwing together pasta with their bare hands.

It was very, very hectic. As a server, the point was to be

able to take a lot of tables at once so you could make the most money possible. But, trying to give ten tables good service is *im*possible. You need to be able to spend more time with each table. At Pao Pao we were to take five tables at a time. At this new place I was given the entire patio by myself, or the entire back room, which was thirty or so tables. I had anxiety attacks on those days. I would get terrible chest pains and my eyes would fill with tears. I would see four tables of people with their menus down, ready to order. I would then see three or four *other* tables irate, because their food was taking so long. Their food was ready, I just didn't have an extra second to go and get it! Then I would see four additional tables that were ready to pay. Some needed change, some needed their credit card run. Then there would be a few other tables that were done and were ready for their check. And there was always a table with a baby that needed some special request- some cut up oranges, some plain spaghetti with butter. Some peas. And all of these people were staring at me. I had to just avoid making eye contact. It was called being "slammed" if you were really busy (and "dead" if you were slow.)

Many famous people came into that particular restaurant, everyone from Mr. T to Lisa Marie Presley. I waited on Will Smith and Jada Pinkett, Tommy Lee and Pamela Anderson, Rick James, Alice Cooper, Tito Jackson, Mick Fleetwood, Alec Baldwin and Kim Basinger, and probably forty other famous people, at least. I was most excited to see the one-armed drummer from Def Leppard though, and anyone from *The Brady Bunch* made me star struck. One time I was waiting on Rebecca Romijn and John Stamos- she was really cool, ordering a ton of food and he was cranky and on a strict diet. He was annoyed that she could eat whatever she wanted and she was cracking up. He asked me what kind of mustard we had, and I named off four different types, one of them being a brand called Beaver. He said, in all seriousness, "Is the beaver hot?" and then he heard her stifling laughter. He slowly looked over at her with a totally straight face and she laughed even harder- she couldn't stop. I started laughing with her, and then *I* couldn't stop and he just sat there and gave her the side eye.

There were also a lot of wannabe actors that frequented the place, which meant many "don't you know who I am" special requests. I expected it from the women, but it was pathetic to hear so many men want diet food. They were SUCH pussies. Basically, no one in the whole town would eat anything touched by oil or butter. Southern California- of course. Of course. No butter, no oil, everything steamed, and everything well done so all fat is off it. Understood. That is how Pao Pao was too. But the people at this place wanted well done egg whites, scrambled with steamed broccoli with a well toasted sesame bagel sliced in threes. *Threes.* Not sliced down the middle, but sliced *three times.* Even the things that were most simple were made complicated. They wanted such specific things; it just couldn't be done sometimes. And they would throw a fit: yell, throw their food, call you stupid- there was nothing too crazy for these people to do.

One demanding woman wanted well-done, sunny side up eggs with no oil/butter. The cook tried to do it, but she kept sending it back. He finally said he couldn't make it any more well done. People would want bacon that "shattered." They thought that if it were really well done, there would be no fat on it. Little did they know the secret to making it that well done was to deep fry it.

The entertainment industry assholes absolutely refused to order off the huge menu. No, that was for common folk. They liked the thought of a chef personally preparing something for them. They would shut the menu and say, "I feel like two turkey slices, with a well toasted slice of sourdough, a side of cantaloupe and a side or carrots. I would like two spinach leaves steamed for three minutes, placed on top of the bread." They were always telling us how many minutes something was to be cooked, things like that. Little did they know the chef was hung-over and on coke, with a cigarette hanging out of his mouth and did not give a fuck about any of the screaming people. He was never impressed by any star (except for when John Ritter came in.) He had tired eyes, and didn't say much. Never got excited. Life seemed to be over for him, except for the weekends, when he would hire hookers and strippers to come to his place and do coke with him. That is what he looked forward to.

The other cook was fat, had gold teeth, and always dry-humped the air in front of him and while singing Mexican love songs. If I yelled at him over a wrong order, he would say, "Are you red? Are you *red*?!" meaning, 'Are you on your period? 'Cause your being a bitch.' If I started gaining weight, he would always say, "No more *cheese* hah-ney; you are getting *fat*." If one of the waitresses asked for their order and it was there in front of them, which happened often because there were plates everywhere, he would yell, "OPEN YOUR FUCKIN' OJOS HAH-NEY!"

The deep fryer guy was also always on coke. He was

young, had a lazy eye, short curly hair, and was always laughing. Sometimes he would slide a little folded up piece of paper over the counter while I was waiting for my food. I would open it to see white powder and quickly fold it back up and throw it at him and say, "Are you *crazy*? Someone is going to *see* you!"

The staff was very cool though, and I recall paying some of the young bus boys to rub my feet after my shift. Oh, and I got in trouble for being rude a few times. Once a guy wouldn't get off his phone and I finally asked him for his number so I could call him and take his order- my boss was not too happy about that. Another time a huge table of loud Arab businessmen spent a few hundred dollars on food and tried to leave me a five dollar bill for a tip. I looked at it and then put out my other hand and motioned for more, with a bored look on my face. I said, "Come on guys, cough it up." They were FURIOUS. They snatched the five dollar bill, ripped it to pieces, screamed and yelled…and then gave me more money.

I dated a younger guy from work who was convinced he looked just like Brad Pitt. He *did* look a lot like him, but I refused to admit it, just because I saw how much he wanted me to say it. We never discussed it, but he would do the stupidest things, such as asking me to go to the video store with him and then picking up Brad Pitt movies, hoping I would say, "Hey…you look just like Brad Pitt!" He even went and stood next to a poster of Brad Pitt in *Twelve Monkeys*. I still wouldn't say it. I acted as if it hadn't dawned on me.

He desperately wanted me to try Ecstasy with him, which I did, and it did nothing to me. He was dancing around me with a glow stick and some nasal spray that was supposed to increase my high and I was just sitting there trying not to laugh. The most fantastic thing that happened with him was when I was at his apartment and his beauty pageant ex-girlfriend (who was probably a current girlfriend) kept banging on the door and he wanted me to hide. I said, please, I don't *hide.* I am not crouching in some *closet* so you can hide from some chick in a tiara and a sash. He was begging me, telling me she was crazy. I examined my nails on the couch and refused to budge. The girl's banging was getting more and more intense; she started yelling that she knew he was home. I could see her through the foggy glass window- it was one of those big windows that is like a shower door, you can't really see through it, but light comes through and all of that. The girl backed up, took a running leap, and shattered the entire glass window with her body. After she did a total stuntman move, she ran straight into his room to try to slap him or something; it was like the glass was just a minor inconvenience. He grabbed her and tried to carry her out but she was kicking and flailing all over the place. She somehow clamped her legs into the doorframe and he couldn't get her out. It was a spectacular sight. I sat there all calm with my eyebrows up while all of this commotion was going on.

***

That August was a big deal because Birdie was finally turning twenty-one. I had a birthday card set out for her, which I was sure she would love. I ran into one of the Jesus Twins at work, who Birdie and I called the "Twin Idiots." They were two obnoxious New York guys with inflated egos who were often on The Howard Stern Show. We used to see them at the Rainbow and they would totally annoy us. I had the one twin write a special note t

her on his show flier and I included it in the card.
I couldn't wait for her to open it! The phone rang the next
morning before I left for work. Charlie answered and said
it was for me; it was a guy. I was excited and nervous-
oooh, who could it be?

I plopped down on her bed and said hello. I heard the
voice of someone who was quiet and sad. He announced
himself as Birdie's boyfriend. He had been seeing her the
whole year I was in Colorado.

"Yes?" I said.

"Birdie...she died," he said quietly.

"Wait...*What*?"

"...She's dead."

I couldn't comprehend it for a second. He told me she
overdosed on heroin. Her heart had stopped. He started
crying and told me the funeral was in a few days. I was
completely devastated. I wondered if she had done it on
purpose.

The first thing that hit me was that I could never talk to her
again. Never see her again. Never laugh with her again.
From that point on I went into a horrible, horrible sinking
depression. I was sure I could never laugh again for the
rest of my life, never smile again. There was no way the
heaviness could leave my heart.

The boyfriend picked me up and took me to her parent's

house before the funeral, and her mother told me to take anything I wanted from her room. I went upstairs to the room by myself. The lights were off and there was a little bit of sunlight coming through the window. It looked so *small* suddenly. It was unusually quiet without her laugh and her music and her hairdryer. All of her walls were still covered with pictures of models from French and Italian *Vogue,* yet there were some stuffed animals and things from her childhood out on shelves. She was part kid, part woman. I looked at the pink recliner. I sat in that thing for *hours* waiting for her to get ready. Hours! And when guys tried to come home with us, we would say, "Sorry, there is no room for you, you will have to sleep on the pink chair" as a joke. She died in that chair. It hurt my heart, made my chest sting.

I remembered how relieved I used to be to come to her house when I lived in miserable conditions with my father. I opened her closet and looked at all of her pretty clothes. I felt sick thinking that her body was…gone. I took a few pictures from her photo albums and left the room. On the way down the stairs, I saw her old dog. The damn thing outlived her, which freaked me out.

As we all walked out to go to the service, her dad made a comment that we all looked good and she would have liked that. I sat with the boyfriend during the service and could barely look up at the collage someone had made next to her casket. It felt like a dream, like it couldn't be real. Her parents went up to view the body and her mother started crying, bent down, and kissed her. Then the boyfriend went up to kiss her and started crying because her lips were so cold. He was absolutely in shock. I started to go up and midway I stopped, turned around and booked it out of the church in front of everyone. I didn't care; I couldn't look at her dead. She would not have wanted me to look at her like that.

Everyone soon came outside for the burial. They had a guy playing the bagpipes while they lowered her into the ground. I just remember losing it, I couldn't stop crying, and I thought I would be sick. I propped myself against a tree. Her mother came over and tried to comfort me, which made me feel worse for making a scene.

Journal Entry 8/16/1997

Today was Birdie's funeral. I couldn't handle seeing her casket. It was the freakiest, most terrible thing that I have ever seen in my life. Her mom said she didn't have to worry about her anymore. Her dad said she was always one step ahead of them. Her parents didn't want the Hollywood people knowing about it, but I did see this girl Laura in one of the pews. She was the one person Birdie thought of when she wanted to pretend she was dead once. She said, "Do you think Laura would come to my funeral if I ever died? Will you call her and say I died and see what she does?" I told her she was an idiot and no, I would not do that. Well, she would have been happy because there sat Laura, probably the only person besides me from the Hollywood crowd who attended. Her parents wouldn't let anyone notify her drug related friends like Ashley Allesandro, who someone has since told and who is now a basket case.

*How could she be...how could she not be alive? I never expected five years ago, that out of all of those crazy people, I would be at **her** funeral. Nothing ever happened* *to any of us. I have always told myself that as long as Birdie and Anthony are still standing, then I can go on partying and living the way I do and I have nothing to worry about.*

She was very caught up in that party scene and was not interested in trying to make the conversion to a normal life, or even a semi-normal one like I have. I tried so many times to talk her into pulling herself together but she wasn't interested. The very last time I spoke to her was a few months ago. My old roommate Simon called me and said that she and her man were very strung out. I was very worried- I called her and talked to her and she laughed and said she was fine. She was hanging out with Ashley, her former rival from Hollywood; they had joined forces as all pretty girls eventually do. We talked for a while. At least I told her how much I loved her. I told her I wanted to write a book about her life one day and she said I could. Then the strangest thing happened when I hung up. I knew she was going to die. I started crying really hard at my aunt's house because something told me that she was going to die soon. I told my aunt and she was like, "But she isn't dead- you just talked to her." Well, I couldn't explain it, but something told me I wouldn't talk to her again, that she would be dead. And now she is.

I loved that girl, deep in my heart. I honestly really loved her, so much, no matter what she did. I was going to send her a card for her twenty-first birthday tomorrow, but I just crumbled it up and threw it in the trash. I wish she could've seen it. She will never see anything ever again. She is gone. I can't talk to her. I can't see her. I loved her so much. I wonder if she can see me. I wonder if God took her because her mother prayed so many times. I don't know if I can ever be happy again.

I could not shake it. In a stroke of irony, I saw the Dandy
Warhols' new video to "Not If You Were the Last Junkie
on Earth." There were dancing syringes doing high kicks
against a pink background and a mime vomiting. The
words of the song seemed like a cruel joke. I sat on the
couch with snot running down my nose. I felt sick to my
stomach. I thought someone had been spying on my brain,
on our lives. The timing was just weird- I had never heard
such a blatant song about heroin.

Then I started getting phone calls. People were asking me
what happened but I felt that she wouldn't want me to say
anything. I didn't know how to handle it. When I went out
to places that we used to frequent together, such as The
Gate, I would get questions and I refused to acknowledge
her death. It seemed too sensational and gossipy. I just said
she was fine, never better, doing great, jet-setting
somewhere.

Charlie gave me a few days to be sad over Birdie's death
and then she asked when I would be over it so we could
have fun again. I told her I was trying, but I couldn't shake
it yet. We ended up parting ways and were never friends
again.

I moved in with some girls from work and all I wanted to
do was snort a ton of coke. I didn't want to *think* about
anything. I just wanted to feel better. I was jonesing for it
all the time, but couldn't afford the good stuff. I settled for
the cheap shit that Carrie Ann had: glass. I don't even
know what the hell that even *is,* but I snorted it. I think it is
crystal meth mixed with like, rat poison and powdered

laundry soap, I don't know. But it made looking at wallpaper for three hours, fun. And yes, I looked at wallpaper for three hours once. It was some bottom of the barrel, terrible drug that people did in trailer parks. I remember going to work without sleeping a wink. My pupils were so big that my eyes were pure black- no blue was showing. I managed to do my job on that shit. The managers noticed and were like, *have you **slept** yet?* They knew.

I had heard about all of the bad things drugs did to you. Kill your brain cells, ruin your body and all of that. But there was something else that I hadn't heard of, and I found out about it during a romantic evening with one of the hottest guys in town. Hot Guy did drugs- I guess you could say he was a hot loser- you know the type. They are the type you are supposed to stay away from, but you often don't, at least in your twenties. I was at Hot Guy's house, eating pineapple candy with him and making out. In between making out, we were snorting God knows what- probably some rat poison or arsenic- I didn't even *ask.*

All was going well (for a night in the Valley at least,) until my stomach started rumbling. Suddenly, I felt that my ass was going to explode like a volcano. I clenched my butt cheeks and ran to the bathroom, one that was unfortunately within close earshot of Hot Guy, and had a case of crazy drug diarrhea. I came out of the bathroom twenty minutes later and he was suddenly tired and had to be somewhere. I left in total embarrassment. I didn't hear from him again, but I did receive an unusual crank call: I answered the phone and all I heard was a toilet flushing. Served me right, I guess.

I was very paranoid about death that whole year. It was a terrible phobia and something that bothered me to the point of crying. What *happened* to Birdie? Where did she *go*? Didn't The Bible say you couldn't go to heaven if you killed yourself? Or was that just the words of a religion and not The Bible? Could she really be in *hell*? She wasn't a bad person inside. That wouldn't be fair. Was she in some waiting room in the sky? Was she just in a peaceful sleep? It bothered me deeply that she wasn't around and I had no idea where she went. It took me a while to get over the shock. I think the thing that finally made me calm down a little bit was a dream I had. It was Birdie and me in a car, tearing around windy canyons. She told me she was happy she met me on her journey. I felt a little better. I had more dreams about her in very fast cars, dreams where I told her to slow down, slow down, you're driving too fast, this is dangerous. I had a dream that I was trying to carry her on a bicycle, with all of her luggage. I couldn't get anywhere with her and her stuff on my back. I had to drop her off so I could move forward. I had to leave her behind.

Then I had dreams about myself: I was on a freeway and cars were passing me by. I was crawling alongside the freeway in a bed of thorns. I had to get to my destination but it was so much harder for me because I didn't have the same means of transportation as all of the others. I had dreams I was on the freeway on my bike, trying to pedal fast enough to keep up and I was too slow. People were zooming by and I was being left in the dust.

One of the waitresses at work became pregnant. She was totally calm, happy, and mellow. But as her stomach started to grow, I started to panic. *I cannot let this happen to me. I cannot stay here. This is just not okay. What if I want kids one day? I can't be here when I am pregnant. I need to get out of here.* I knew I could do better, but I had no marketable skills to go anywhere else. What was I going to do, tell them I was fabulous? That wasn't going to fly. I was getting older. I needed some sort of a plan. I started feeling a lot of stress. I wore polyester pants, dirty shoes and smelled like grease. I always felt disgusting. My life was an unhappy one. I kept breaking down and crying. The other waitresses were wondering why I was acting so crazy. They told me to calm down, just deal with it, it was just a *job*. I couldn't explain it to them. As a kid, I had always imagined that I would become something great. I had high hopes for myself. I knew I was capable of more. There is nothing worse than not living up to your potential, than letting yourself down. It is a horrible feeling to know you are not growing, you are not learning, you are doing *nothing* to better yourself. Those things didn't mean anything to me in the years before, but as I grew older, it just...*bothered* me.

I didn't have any plan for my life except to make it through the day each day. I felt completely lost. I started looking around for a mentor, someone who could advise me. I went to a girl at work named Robbie who had a journalism degree. *She will know what to do,* I thought. We went out to lunch and she told me I needed to work on a resume. Resume? What the hell would I *put* on the damn thing? I felt scared.

I turned twenty-five the next year, and moved out into my own apartment. I put my mattress on the living room floor in front of the TV. I was too scared to sleep in my room, I was afraid someone would break in through the living room windows and kill me, so I thought I would be able to hear better if I just slept in the living room. My room had nothing in it. Just a few boxes of old journals and books from my grandmother's garage. There were several other boxes that had my name on them, but I wasn't sure what was in them. When I opened them, I saw that they were all of my old toys and belongings from when I was a child. Strawberry Shortcake dolls, sticker books, lunch boxes. I lined them all up in the living room of my empty apartment, sat with them, and cried. I missed being little. So much. I didn't want anyone to come to my apartment so I could just leave the big Strawberry Shortcake pie shop in the living room. It was as if my heart burst wide open.

Living on my own with no roommates to fall back on, made me into a functioning member of society. I had to pay my rent on time, pay my bills on time- cable, phone, electric and gas. I didn't really buy food because I ate free at the restaurant. I never rang in my food because the cooks would make me whatever I wanted. I never had any savings, so it was scary to think I wasn't prepared for an emergency. It was a huge burden when I had to buy my yearly boxes of contact lenses. I always had to save up.

They say a real friend is one who walks in when the rest of the world walks out. One of the only people who remained from my previous life, was my friend Allison, from Pao Pao. She always invited me to the holidays at her parent's house. I was so grateful to have her as a friend. She took on something that needed to be addressed, but that was a touchy subject. I needed to learn social etiquette and manners. It wasn't something that just anyone could approach.

She would tell me about her parents and their friends and

what they did and didn't do- kind of a little crash course in how not to be white trash. She was very gentle about it. I learned that I was in fact very tacky and abrasive much of the time and went about things a little rough. Oh, okay, who am I kidding- I was really rough. I was a bull in a china shop. I snapped at people, was ready to fight at the drop of a hat. If you came and tapped me on the shoulder, I would turn around with my dukes up.

Allison was a tough girl herself, but she had a British mother who taught her proper manners and protocol. If she needed to use that shit, she could pull it out and have tea with the Queen Mother without batting an eyelash. Needless to say, she showed me how to behave in many social situations. She taught me to be polite, how to be gracious and how to have more empathy toward people. She told me about having pride in yourself, in your family name. There was loyalty in her family. I was beginning to understand just how important that was.

She explained to me about keeping your word. When you said you were going to do something, you needed to do it. When you said you were going to be somewhere, you went, period. You went to any length for a friend or a family member. You had to be there for people.

Allison had grown in her own right since I first met her. She was very warm, compassionate, and intelligent. She was there to talk to me about my fears, my sadness over my family and my depression over Birdie. She spent hours talking to me, coming over to my place, inviting me over there. She thought I was so great. She was always telling me I was smart and funny. She made me feel really good. She believed in me so much, gave me so much encouragement, so many pep talks. I am talking hours and hours' worth of support. She was also patient with me when I snapped at her and dealt with her in less than civil ways.

I took some time to myself, just thinking and soaking it all in. I wrote in journals and sat by myself a lot. I felt things shifting in my mind. I felt I wanted to step up to the plate; I was truly ready to take action.

One day I looked up into the sky and said to God, "I am ready."

Seventeen

WHAT BECAME OF ME

Here is what became of me:

The first thing that happened was that I immediately met the man who was to become my husband, and we started dating. We were both broke and didn't know what we were going to do with our lives, but we fell in love. The second thing that happened was that I realized I was in dire need of therapy, which was expensive. I paid for it in cash, with my tips. Then I started attending church- that one was the hardest of all. I wanted to strengthen my relationship with God, but I felt as if I would be struck by lightning even entering the building. I told God I would never do drugs again, and I never did. I am sure you want more of an explanation than that, but that was really it- I made that decision and stuck to it.

I saved up some money and took some computer classes to

build my skills. I then went to a temp agency and they were cool enough to let me come in an hour before work every day and do tutorials on their computers, free of charge. I took tons of notes on the computer programs. I had a yellow tablet filled with directions on how to use them. I never went out on the assignments they offered me, because it was always only a day or two, and I needed a real job, where I could pay my bills.

I asked my journalist friend at work if I could pick her brain about careers. She sat me down and told me to go to UCLA to take some night classes. UCLA? I mean...How could I even get in there? She explained they offered special programs called "Extension" classes. You could just pay the fee for the class and go. I didn't need to be accepted to the school, or pay a huge tuition. She asked me a bunch of questions and told me it sounded like I should go out for Public Relations. I signed myself up and asked questions later.

I was petrified to drive out to UCLA and walk on to the campus. I didn't know where anything was, I didn't know what to wear...I was so scared! I thought they would laugh me out of there. I was floored that my legs were moving me across the beautiful manicured lawns. I couldn't believe it. I found parking. I found my class in the beautiful old buildings. I sat down amongst the other students and felt okay. I liked the instructor, Jeff DuClos who was from Rogers and Cowan, a very prominent PR firm. The class sounded interesting when he explained what it would be about. As it went on, I found I really liked the class. I felt challenged, which made me overjoyed. I felt like I was doing something I could be proud of. I did reports on things I was interested in, did research and spoke in front of the class.

I took six or seven more classes. They were mostly communication and writing classes. How to deal with different types of people. One of them was crisis and reputation management, one was writing for the press, one was publicity management. There were a bunch of neat classes with great speakers that came in and taught us how to gently let people down if you didn't like something, how to get people on the phone, how to get someone to read your email, how to deal with people in meetings, how to get someone to pay attention to your project. It was a crash course in business, plain and simple. I was starting to accumulate skills that could be used at a real job. I remember when I left the school and was tearing down Sunset to the 405 in the dark, I would scream with happiness. My heart was filled with pride and joy.

I went to the UCLA bookstore and bought a book on job interviews and studied every question and what a good answer would be. I realized after reading it that I had been going about my past interviews all wrong. I had had no clue. I couldn't believe I had ever gotten a job with the things I used to say on interviews! I put together a pathetic resume and Allison took it to someone she knew at a big corporation. The next thing I knew, I had an interview.

I HAD to ace it. I had to. I was dying, just *dying* to get out of the restaurant business. They were about to fire me for a bad attitude. I couldn't even *pretend* any more. I wanted to leave so desperately. Two women interviewed me a few days later. I was so happy just to be there, I was beaming. I almost did a kick ball change and some jazz hands. They asked many of the questions that were in the book I studied, so I had prepared answers. I said the right things! *Me!* I got a call later that day. It was a job offer! I fell into a heap on the floor because I couldn't believe it. It was all over. I was no longer a waitress.

I was determined, more determined than I have ever been in my entire life, to make something of myself. I vowed I would not fuck up this chance. Most people hated offices; but I was thrilled to walk into one. I was so happy to be away from screaming kids and club sandwiches. If my job was taping paper together, then dammit, I was going to be the best paper taper known to man. The average was 50 per hour? I would do 75. I felt so lucky to be at a place where there was chance of actual advancement and a chance to have a career.

I studied the professional look. It was a new creation, just like the others I had created. I knew I had one shot to get it right. I had to look the part. I opened a charge card at a really boring store and bought three pencil skirts in black, grey, and camel. Then I bought three collared shirts- white, black and grey, that went with the skirts. I went and bought some good shoes, a camel pair and a black pair, closed toe, not too high. I eventually accumulated a beautifully groomed wardrobe. I was completely overdressed for my position. I dressed nicer than the managers did. I had mainly female managers, so I hid any part of me that would not be deemed professional, or that would cause another female to not like me or want to compete with me or take me down out of jealousy. That meant wearing my long hair up in a perfect bun every single day, hiding my figure, not dressing cute or stylish, and appearing very conservative at all times.

I knew I was doing something right because my co-workers tried to give me shit. One older woman told me, "Don't bother dressing up- it doesn't matter, you'll never get promoted here. I have been here for *years*. Nobody sees us here. You might as well be comfortable." She looked like refried hell every day in sweats, moping around and smoking cigarettes. It was true; everyone was in jeans and sweats. We were not visible to any executives. They were in the main headquarters across town in a showy, new high-rise building with marble lobbies, elevators, and people in suits. We were in a rundown warehouse, really. A crappy one story building in an industrial area, littered with trash, near porn studios. The place was not visible to the big wigs.

I tried to remain positive. I read a book called "How to Be a CEO" which touched on the positive attitude and other traits of a CEO. I started to buy tons of other books on business etiquette, speech, climbing a corporate ladder and taking initiative. I studied those books relentlessly. I was determined to crack the code of moving up that corporate ladder. The books told me things I had never even considered; from do not lean against anything to do not wear perfume because you risk offending someone who doesn't like the scent- you could lose a client. Have a firm but not too firm of a handshake, all that stuff. I studied the language of business and the pitfalls women often make (don't say, "I *feel* that we should blah blah blah- leave feelings out of business.) I read books on how to play 'hardball' in business, how to formally dine with clients, how to shine in meetings, how to deal with difficult people, how to get noticed on a team, how to this and how to that- I read every single book I could get my manicured hand on (no French tips or loud colored nails- only short, very light pale pink nails!) I studied business writing. I took every single class the company offered and posted all of the certificates in my cubicle. While my co-workers had Winnie the Pooh coffee mugs, cut out comic strips, kitten calendars and pictures of their kid everywhere, I had a very deliberate set created. A row of books. A green desk lamp. One small plant (ivy.) An American flag.

I was friendly to everyone (but not too friendly- didn't want to be seen as a social butterfly and not taken seriously) and did my work as perfect and as quickly as possible. I continued studying every aspect of being promotable. I joined special groups and teams to try to gain visibility. I volunteered for special projects. I wrote for the newsletter. I was never late to the job. I never called in sick, unless I was dying. I never left early. Every move was calculated and designed for promotion. I just remember always saying, "Sure, I can do that," and then running to the phone and calling Allison and asking her things like how to use a fax machine or a copier. She walked me through every single thing.

I sat at my computer and learned every single program and short cut that was available. Lazy I was no longer. I did everything I could as excellent as I could and kept my eye on the prize. I didn't know what I wanted to do as my next position- I had no idea what half of the positions even *entailed*. I just knew I had to get to the next position above the one I was in, whatever it was. It's stapling two pieces of shit together? Fine, I'll take the job and be the best shit stapler there is, as long as it makes more money and gets me one more step up the ladder. I was totally psycho.

After about six months, I got a small raise- 30 cents or

something like that. Then, about six months later, I got another little raise and changed positions. I excelled at that job and tried for a position a little higher up. My co-workers still insisted that the most you could get was a fifty-cent increase a year. I thought…no, not me. This is *me* we're talking about. I don't read just one book on a subject, I read fifteen. I didn't play house as a girl. I ran an empire. I took everything I ever did and ran with it. Even being a loser, I couldn't just be sort of a loser. I was a *monumental* loser! So scoot the fuck out of the way and let me hurry up and take over this entire company, okay?

A year passed. I was making more than the people around me due to some extra merit increases here and there. Some of the higher-ups felt that I was moving too fast. I was called in for a meeting with the Director of Something or Other. She said that she didn't feel I was ready to move up any further and if I were to do so, it could only harm me. She didn't want to 'set me up to fail.' Set me up to *fail*? I smiled serenely with my hands in my lap, legs crossed at the ankle. I eyeballed her Weight Watchers bars, her Disney mug, her calendar of cute animals, and her outfit from Lane Bryant. I assured her that I was not *going* to fail, thanked her for her concern, and went on my merry way. The path wouldn't be through her, I was going to have to move around her.

There was finally an opening in the big, visible, high-rise headquarters location. I immediately applied, interviewed and was hired for a bigger position. I excelled at the job and asked for the hardest accounts they had. Next thing I knew, I was managing million-dollar accounts for the company.

I got another raise. Then another. Then *another*. Two years later, I was in a management position in that high-rise building. I had taken my boss's job. I was in charge of a team of twelve people, some of them my former co-workers. A few had college degrees and were far more educated than I was. But they didn't have the drive I had: part balls, part determination and a dash of crazy.

I continued to study business and coached many people on my team on interviewing for higher positions, how to represent themselves professionally, how to move up and make more money.

I saw that Director of Something or Other in the elevator one day. I smiled serenely once again. I knew that she was aware of my staggering growth in the company and the new position I held. I barreled right past her and her "advice." She knew it and **I** knew it. As someone who I can't remember once said, "The greatest pleasure in life is doing what people say you cannot do."

I ended my career at the big corporation four years after my start date. If I had listened to the women around me, I would have made only two more dollars an hour than when I started. Instead, I was salaried and had increased my earnings by exactly one hundred percent. I left that job for another company at a Fortune 500 company ,who offered me five figures more a year than I was making.

I was determined to continue on my quest to better myself. I read so many books that my eyes nearly fell out. I read classic literature, studied politics, world history, and current events. I also read countless books on psychology, especially on alcoholic families and families of addicts. I studied etiquette book after etiquette book until I was having dreams about table settings and proper introductions. In hindsight, it was certainly overkill. But coming from the life I did? I just *needed* it. I wanted that formal training. I wanted to feel prepared in any social situation. I never wanted to turn down a job because I was afraid of the people around me. I never wanted to avoid walking into a room of established people because I felt inferior. I never wanted to be nervous dining at a table with someone important. I never wanted to feel uncomfortable walking into an upscale store. I wanted to make sure I could hold a conversation with anyone, anywhere.

I was falling more and more in love with the man I was to marry, who had grown in his own career during the time I had grown in mine. He proposed to me and we were married the next year in a big church wedding. We bought a place and decided to get all new stuff. We threw out every crappy thing from my old apartment: mismatched silverware, years of hand me downs, scratched dressers, stained couches, 1970's tables, chipped cups, old towels... I threw them all away. We bought beautiful new things. A soft comfortable couch with tons of Italian wool pillows. Thick crystal vases filled with white flowers. Smooth beautiful plates and fat glasses and a huge, clean, stainless steel fridge. No more moldy, used fridge. Beautiful cherry wood office furniture. Thick monogrammed towels in the bathroom. New soft sheets and blankets and plushy pillows on the bed.

I was stunned at my new life, making snow angels in my new sheets. I was in love, happy, and proud of myself. Soon I had a little golden baby, quit working, and we moved to the beach, right by the ocean. Are you sick to your stomach yet, of my good luck? Well, don't be.

Within a year I found a lump in my breast that turned out to be stage two breast cancer. And I did the strongest chemotherapy treatments available. I was sitting there in the chemo place with a bunch of old people, thinking, "What am I *doing* here?"

Talk about getting comfortable with yourself, try looking at yourself *bald.*

I am not ready to write about cancer. I just can't. Not yet. All I can say is that it took me shaving the rest of my hair off, the clumps that were left after the chemo killed the rest, to look myself in the eyes and love myself. I finally looked at the real me. I looked into my own eyes, into my own soul. I saw a woman who wasn't just hair and makeup. I saw a strong person who I respected and admired.

As I write this, my hair has just grown in long enough for me to finally be done with wigs. And I haven't given up.

You are now reading my book, which brings me to the last thing I am going to say, dear reader:

As the saying goes,

"It is never too late to become the person you were meant to be."

CPSIA information can be obtained
at www.ICGtesting.com
Printed in the USA
LVHW110214280520
656788LV00001B/113

9 780615 487373